Also by Dr. Charles Foster

Truth Without Fear: How to Communicate Difficult News in Tough Situations

Parent/Teen Breakthrough: The Relationship Approach (with Mira Kirshenbaum)

What Do I Do Now?

*Dr. Foster's 30 Laws of
Great Decision Making*

Charles Foster, Ph.D., M.B.A.

Simon & Schuster

New York London Toronto Sydney Singapore

SIMON & SCHUSTER
Rockefeller Center
1230 Avenue of the Americas
New York, NY 10020

SIMON & SCHUSTER and colophon are registered trademarks
of Simon & Schuster, Inc.

Designed by Brady McNamara

Manufactured in the United States of America

10   9   8   7   6   5   4   3   2   1

Library of Congress Cataloging-in-Publication Data

Foster, Charles.
    What do I do now?: Dr. Foster's 30 laws of great decision making /
Charles Foster.
        p.   cm.
    Includes index.
        1. Decision making. I. Title.

BF448.F67 2001
153.8'3—dc21   00-063729

ISBN 0-684-86919-5

To my wonderful daughters, Rachel and Hannah,
and to the youthful part in all of us
that insists on making new beginnings

Special Thanks

I T was my father who planted the seed for this book. It began the day he died, in my arms. He was an old man, and although he'd accomplished many things he knew he'd made some bad decisions. I was very young then, and I didn't have a track record of many good decisions to look back on either. Facing death, he was afraid for me. All he wanted was to know that I would go on to make good decisions. That was his last request. I promised him I would.

His request was a burden, but it was also a great gift. "Make good decisions." That would be the key to unlock every door. The light that would illuminate the path I took, starting that day twenty-four years ago.

It was because I took my promise to my father seriously that I began the quest to discover just what we need, you and I, to make great decisions and never, ever again make a bad decision.

My father started me down the path, but I've had many guides along the way. I particularly want to thank all the men and women who in one way or another participated in the research for this book. They gave me a great gift by telling me the stories of their lives. Even more, they let me witness the hopes and agonies they went through in the process of making big, tough decisions. And with incredible generosity they showed me the naked truth of how their decisions turned out.

Mira Kirshenbaum and I have been full, fifty/fifty partners in everything we've written. This book is no exception. We wrote it together. Every word here is as much Mira's as it is mine. I can remember back thirty-five years ago to when we first met, and we were just teenagers. We talked about our futures, and even then, more girl than woman, Mira understood in her bones that life was a series of choices, that you could almost always choose what would happen to you, and that choosing well meant living well. This book is a testament to everything she's cared about most. And in that way this book has been Mira's gift to me.

I have so may colleagues, friends, and teachers to thank that I'm in a quandary. Detailed thanks would require a book. A mere list of names would turn individuals into a crowd—plus I'd be terrified of leaving someone out. The people who have contributed to this know who they are, and they have been personally thanked. But my vision would have been blocked if I'd not been able to stand on their shoulders.

One name, however, must be singled out: Professor Tom Dunn of Harvard Business School and Boston College Graduate School of Management. It was Tom who showed me, at the very highest level of decision making, how the simple transcends the complicated, how a few essentials always lie at the heart of a mare's nest of inessentials, and how basic principles—the right ones, of course—always produce better results than elaborate procedures.

I have been enormously grateful to discover that I have a jewel of an editor in Sydny Miner. She could not have been more supportive or more in sync with what this book is trying to accomplish. Every step along the way Sydny has been brilliant and has pushed to make wonderful things happen.

Thanks also to all the other terrific people at Simon & Schuster. A totally first-class operation. I'm particularly grateful to Victoria Meyer for her continuing efforts to make sure that everyone who could possibly benefit from this book has it brought to their attention. And thanks to Michael Accordino, Andrea Mullins, Brady McNamara, Sam Kittman, and the totally excellent copy editor who not only put up with but enhanced my "casual" prose.

Finally, heartfelt thanks to my wonderful agent, Bob Tabian, who, quite simply, made this book happen.

Charles Foster

Contents

What Do I Do Now?

Dr. Foster's 30 Laws of
Great Decision Making

"I'll Never Make a
Bad Decision Again"

H ERE you are, heroically facing a big decision. Maybe it's a de-cision you've been agonizing over. Maybe it's a decision that will change your life. Maybe you're trying to make a number of decisions all at once. You just can't figure out what you should do now.

Your decision could be about anything at all—quitting a job or starting a new career. Ending a relationship or making a commit-ment to a person. Starting a business. Wondering whether to start that business in Topeka or Tashkent. Having a baby. Putting a rela-tive in a nursing home. Starting fertility treatments. Going for plas-tic surgery. Retiring early. Moving. Going halvesies with your sister on a lakeside cottage. *Anything.*

"What do I do now?" is one of your questions. But there's an-other deeper question haunting almost everyone facing a decision that's important: "Do I have what it takes to make the best deci-sion for me?"

I want you to know that you do have everything it takes to make a great decision. Here's how I know this.

When faced with a decision, the most important quality win-ners have is that they *care* about making good choices. When con-fronted with a big decision, they think about it and work hard to figure out the best thing to do.

What makes losers losers, more than anything, is that they

make decisions the way a cork in the ocean decides which way it's going to go. They are totally controlled by the haphazard forces around them. They make bad decisions because they don't really care about *making* decisions.

So the fact that you're holding this book in your hands means you're a winner. It doesn't matter if you've found it hard to make decisions in the past. It doesn't matter that maybe you've made some bad decisions. It doesn't matter if you're finding it a struggle to make a particular decision right now.

All that matters is your understanding that good decisions are made—they don't just happen—and your caring enough to try to make them.

And so I have important news for you.

Whatever you're trying to decide, you have everything you need inside you right now to be one of those people who easily, quickly, and comfortably make great decisions.

You just need help seeing what's important for you to pay attention to. Which is exactly what this book was designed to give you: the secrets for making great decisions. The good news is that these secrets are already part of you.

It's easier than you think

I'm just like you. When I started out, I too agonized over my decisions. I was frequently filled with doubt and confusion. Fear of making a bad decision often depressed or paralyzed me. It was hard to trust myself to know what was best to do.

To make matters worse, I thought there was this select group of people who consistently made great decisions quickly and easily. I was jealous, and I felt bad about myself for struggling the way I did.

I suppose I could've stayed stuck forever, feeling I was struggling where others soared. But I got lucky. It just so happened that twenty-five years ago, clients in my psychotherapy and consulting practices started coming to me for help with making decisions.

They were struggling the way I did, and yet they were smart and experienced. To be honest, I felt impatient with them the way I felt impatient with myself. It shouldn't be so hard for any of us to make good decisions, I thought.

I decided to dedicate myself to discovering the ingredients that went into making good decisions. Was it brains? Some mysterious decision-making talent? What?

Discovering secrets

Trying to discover the ingredients, I came across far more than my share of people who consistently, time after time, made good decisions and people who consistently, time after time, made bad decisions. What was the difference between these two groups? What could my research team and I learn that would help people feel confident that they were making better decisions?

We followed two groups of people from all walks of life: twenty-nine men and women who'd made more than their share of bad choices, and thirty-four men and women who'd made more than their share of good choices. For twelve years we monitored the new decisions they made and how they made them. With each person making approximately one big decision a year, I was privileged to witness the conception and birth of about 750 decisions. And I saw how they turned out.

Before I analyzed the results, I was prepared for tough news. I expected that people who made great decisions had some rigorous, complicated procedure they followed that guaranteed them good results, like people who grew perfect lawns.

One thing gave me hope. I knew some very-high-IQ, well-educated people who wouldn't recognize a good decision if it came along and bit them in the butt. And I also knew some people who were less intellectual and educated who, with the ease and confidence of a Zen archery master, could nail a good decision time after time.

Maybe a complicated procedure wasn't the answer after all.

It's easy to do it right

What I discovered was surprising and powerful. When it comes to the kind of decisions you and I agonize over there's no complicated procedure to master. You don't need a big brain. You don't have to go to Harvard. You don't need some special knack, like the ability to put your foot behind your head. You don't even need pencil and paper to write elaborate lists of pros and cons.

What people who make great decisions do is follow a set of simple laws. Nothing complicated. Nothing more than commonsense guidelines that work to produce great decisions. These are the kinds of dos and don'ts that are part of our natural equipment, yours and mine. They feel familiar. Everyone knows them on some level.

The difference between good and bad decision makers? Bad decision makers forget or ignore these laws. Good decision makers let themselves trust these laws that are already part of them.

This means something revolutionary as far as you are concerned. It means that . . .

You are one of the world's great decision makers.

Right now you have everything you need to make great decisions. All you need is to be yourself. The fact is, you were designed by nature to make great choices. Although we are weaker and slower than every other large animal, our advantage lies in being able to find options and choose the best one. If we hadn't been able to do that back when we were wearing leopard skins and carrying clubs, we'd have died out. So your instincts are good. Even if when you look back you feel bad because you've made some poor choices. Even if as you face a big decision now you're feeling scared and overwhelmed.

Decision fear is normal. No matter how smart you are, nothing makes a smart person feel stupid faster than having to make a decision that can take your life in a whole new direction.

This moment of decision holds enormous potential. You're holding your future in your hands. Things could be so great. But things could go so wrong.

Hopes and fears, pros and cons: how quickly we get overwhelmed. If you're facing a big decision, you may feel like a contestant on a game show. If you give the wrong answer you could lose everything. If you could just find the right answer you could win it all.

Real help for real people

The thirty laws you're holding in your hand right now are all the help you need. These are the laws everyday people in the real world follow when they successfully make the kinds of big, tough, confusing decisions we all have to make from time to time.

That's right. No matter what your track record has been, now you too can be one of those people who can count on themselves to make great choices.

We always follow internal laws or rules of some kind no matter what we do. For instance, if you're driving down the highway and see traffic slowing ahead, maybe you follow the rule "Always switch to the fastest-moving lane." Maybe you follow the rule "Stay in your lane and save yourself the stress."

In every area of life, we'd always like to know the best rules of thumb to follow. Now, for the first time, here are the best rules when it comes to making big decisions in life.

Now you'll always know what's best to do

These are the secrets of great decision makers, whether they're prominent or are known as great decision makers only to their friends and family. These secrets will put you in the top 10 percent of decision makers, no matter what your track record.

Why thirty laws? *Because that's how many there are.*

Thousands of maxims and proverbs float around out there. Some are useless: for example, "Never make decisions on Fridays." Some are confusing: "You'll know if it's right for you." Lots will get you into trouble: "Just guess what you'd probably do and do the opposite." *These thirty laws* are the proven winners.

What makes these laws special? *They work.*

These laws are what everyday people facing big, tough choices actually use to make great decisions and to save themselves from making bad ones.

These laws work in the context of our real lives when we're busy, confused, distracted; when it's all too easy to postpone deciding; when it seems everyone you know gives you conflicting advice; when you feel there's no one you can turn to.

These laws work because they are the universal laws. Whatever the specifics of a decision, people who make great decisions apply the universal laws of decision making to their problem.

And these laws work because they're robust, not finicky. Laws that make it possible for people to make great decisions would have to work with flawed, fallible people like you and me. That's wonderful news. You don't have to be brilliant. You don't have to be a control freak. As long as you do your best *with the right tools,* you don't have to do more than that. Believe me, that's more than enough.

What do the thirty laws add up to? I think you'll agree, as you see them, that they add up to these three broad principles:

- *Prudence is a virtue.* Great decision makers are prudent. They may not wear sensible shoes, but they do sensible things.

- *Action is better than inaction.* Great decision makers may look before they leap, but they *do* leap. I expected more delaying tactics among the best decision makers than I found. But they understand that postponing, delaying, avoiding is not good for anyone.

- *Decisions exist to make things wonderful.* Great decision makers want to stay out of trouble like the rest of us, but they understand that most of all you make decisions to make your life wonderful. It's just as easy to make a great decision as it is to make a so-so decision.

What kind of laws are these? *They are intuitive.* Maybe that's the most important point. These laws are not about learning something hard that you've never known before. They are about rediscovering what you've known but have too often forgotten.

Check it out. As you read each law, notice how familiar it

sounds. Connect it with lessons you've already learned. Think about times you've applied this law successfully in the past.

Good decision makers are the same as you. They too have made their share of bad decisions. They too have spent a long time agonizing over difficult decisions. They too have to discover things for themselves by making mistakes. And they too are emotional.

This amounts to an amazing revelation. Those great decision makers? They're not "them." They're you.

You don't become someone who makes good decisions by "learning" these laws. You become the great decision maker you're capable of being by remembering these laws and throwing away all the junk in your head.

Read the thirty laws, and I'll bet you'll have a sense of coming home to truths about life that have been part of your basic equipment for a long time.

Choosing love

I was a teenager when I made the most important decision of my life; there's a lesson for all of us in this story.

It was the summer between my freshman and sophomore years in college. I was living in my first apartment in the East Village in Manhattan. And I had a girlfriend who happened to be away in Mexico for the summer. I felt pretty good about myself.

Then I met the woman who would become my wife. She came into the library where I was working, and I was immediately interested because she was beautiful and because she asked for graduate school catalogues from schools that had good philosophy programs. I was a philosophy major.

We connected immediately. Within days we were inseparable. There was something special between us beyond my wildest dreams.

We met in July. In November, one day before my nineteenth birthday, we were married. That was my great decision: to make a commitment to this woman at a time in my life when doing so made no logical sense. I could've had years and years of fooling around and having fun until I found the "perfect" woman.

Here's the thing: I just sensed that no matter how long I looked I'd never find anyone better. This was not an obvious decision. Guys like me, teenage guys, just didn't say to themselves, "You'll never do any better than this." What we said to ourselves was, "Yeah this chick is great, but you're too young to tie yourself down and who knows if you won't find someone better?"

Part of me wondered if I was making a mistake tying myself down so early. But in fact I was pretty confident. I had one simple notion in my head: if you find someone smart and beautiful and good who likes what you like, you don't blow it.

Almost everything good in my life has flowed from that decision. Teen marriages aren't supposed to work, and usually they don't, but mine did. Thirty-five years later we're still together as happy as ever. I've had infinite moments of gratitude, but never a moment of regret.

It makes me feel faint when I think of how easily I could've screwed up that decision.

Here's the moral of my story. I was as ignorant and inexperienced as any other eighteen-year-old. But even so, I had everything you need to make great decisions. It wasn't luck or talent. Things worked out because intuitively I let myself follow laws I now know everyone follows when they make great decisions.

Sometimes, of course, we get distracted or confused, and so we've made our share of bad decisions. Some of us feel we've made more than our share.

When bad choices happen to good people

No wonder we get scared in the face of a big decision. The bad decisions we've already made lead us to think that we'll keep on making bad decisions.

We've lost our self-trust. And that's the worst loss of all.

The need for self-trust
Boston is a city known for its doctors, and Mike is one of the best. If I had to have open-heart surgery, I'd go to a guy like Mike. An

anesthesiologist who has worked with him told me, "Where Mike shines is when things go wrong. That's the thing about open-heart surgery. The trick is dealing with all the things that go wrong. I've never seen Mike at a loss when this happens."

Outside the operating room it's a completely different story. When the rubber gloves come off, this man of godlike confidence turns into a man with nerves of jelly. Mike thinks there's good reason for him to be so scared. He believes that every nonmedical decision he's ever made was a bad one. Mike thinks he's the kind of guy who buys a car just before Consumers Union issues a report saying it's flunked its crash test.

For a guy who's earned a lot of money, Mike doesn't have much to show. He's lost most of it chasing bad investment tips and paying support to his ex-wives and kids. I'm sure Mike contributed to his relationship problems, but the women he chose were inappropriate for him. All of his friends said so, and they were right.

And Mike's made a lot of bad career choices. Yes, he does have a great reputation, but he hasn't received the academic appointments and the research grants that would make him the world-renowned doctor he could have been.

Now Mike has just been offered a job with an agency sponsored by the World Health Organization, training third-world doctors in the latest techniques. He'd love to do this. It could lead to the type of academic appointment Mike has always wanted.

But Mike may lose this opportunity. He's made so many bad choices in the past he's afraid to choose now. The fact that all signs are favorable means nothing to Mike. In fact he's one step away from becoming a Mr. Opposite—a guy who can trust himself only if he does the opposite of what he thinks he should.

Are you like Mike? Even though you have areas of competence, do you lack self-trust when it comes to making decisions?

Everyone would love to be able to say, "Yes, some decisions are harder to figure out than others, but generally speaking I can trust myself to make really good decisions." *What Do I Do Now?* was written specifically to help you regain your self-trust.

By using these laws to guide your decision making you'll be

able to win the big prize—to make a great decision, yes, to make a great life, sure, but even more, to capture that sense of self-trust in making decisions.

How to use this book

If you're facing a big decision, use the thirty laws as a mental checklist. Go through the laws in order, letting each one have its due impact on you. Each law will shine a powerful spotlight on the one thing that's best for you to do. It might shine a light on an option you've been considering or on a whole new option.

The first ten laws are presented in order of importance. Law #1 comes first because it's the most important. That means it should have the most weight. Law #2 is the second most important. And so on. All together, the first ten are the top ten. Within the remaining twenty laws, all are equally important. You're the final judge as to which laws are most important for you.

Most people use the thirty laws for more than just making a big decision now. They also use them to rebuild their sense of themselves as good decision makers. Every time you read a law, you are growing as a decision maker. So keep dipping into the thirty laws: at bedtime, in the bath, while you're waiting for a plane. Use the laws for a lifetime of support, insight, inspiration, and guidance. They are your passport to a better future.

What's your future made of?

Your future is made of decisions. Great futures are made of great decisions. Why else do you think people have great lives? Luck? Luck comes and goes. Talent? The world is filled with people who have tons of talent but are leading miserable lives. No, people have great lives because they make great decisions.

The fact is that we're all only a couple of good decisions away from a much better future. You have to do it only one step at a time. Your life consists of all the things you say yes to and all the things you say no to. Every yes or no is a decision. A skillful yes to your best option, or a brave no to an alluring but disastrous option, can make a dream come true.

It's true that all the successful people in your life have decided their way to achievement. And a couple of great decisions at the right time can launch your life into the stratosphere. But the biggest payoff from making good decisions isn't success, it's *happiness*.

That's what a track record of good decisions gives you: a life that's what you want it to be, that's trouble free, that works for you, that makes you happy. A life that's your home.

Law #1

Focus on the Most Important Thing

Are you giving full weight to the most important issue?

PEOPLE always ask me, "Okay, there are thirty laws, but is there one that's more important than the others?"

The answer is that the most important law is the one *you* most need to remember as you face your particular decision. But the most important law for shining the biggest spotlight fastest on what's best for you to do is to *focus on the most important thing.*

In spite of its power, this law makes a lot of common sense. Here you are, trying to figure out the best thing to do. You're choosing between a couple of options, and you're weighing many, many factors as you think about what to do. You have your long list of pros and cons. And you're overwhelmed and confused.

Let the five-hundred-pound gorilla have its way

Out of all the things you're juggling and balancing, there's one factor, one consideration, one goal, one issue, one *something* that is truly most important. That is clearly most important. That is overwhelmingly most important.

There you are, juggling and balancing. This law says, cut it out. This law says, hey, you're making things too complicated. Worse, you're forgetting the most important thing. Or if you're not forgetting it, you're forgetting to let it have all the weight it deserves. How much weight is that? A lot more than everything else.

That's the key. *Overweight* the most important thing, under-weight everything else.

A classic dilemma: You're in a boat, and your baby and your dog fall overboard. Whom do you save first? Your baby. You don't juggle the complexities of the exact relative value of a brand-new baby and the dog you've had for years. You just go for the baby.

Well, in every situation and every choice there is some *most important thing,* and the great decision you're capable of begins with your making sure, whatever else you do, that you find it and then give it full weight. Let that most important issue be what it wants to be: the five-hundred-pound gorilla in your decision-making process. That's right. When in doubt let that most important thing dominate your other considerations.

Putting the five-hundred-pound gorilla to work

Focusing on the most important thing is guaranteed to make you a better decision maker. And it's a lot easier to put into practice than you might think.

You may ask, "How will I be able to figure out the one most important thing in making my decision?"

I have a secret for you. People who make great decisions don't sit around agonizing about this question—one can go mad that way. Instead, people who make great decisions just remember to step back from the noisy urgency of the moment and ask themselves, What's the most important thing? Whatever answer they come up with, they make sure it has a huge impact on their decision. They don't make a great decision because they come up with a brilliant, perfect answer. They make a great decision because they remember to ask this most important question.

A new life
Bob was about to graduate from business school. At thirty-seven he was older than most of his classmates, and he had a lot of experience under his belt. Unfortunately most of his experience had consisted of floundering in different jobs he didn't like. Business

school was a way to leverage himself into doing something he cared about and found interesting.

Bob came up with some pretty good post-business-school options. Number one on his list was joining a friend in an internet start-up, providing people customized medical information with links to their doctors and others who might have help or products to offer. His partner had done a lot of work setting up a plan and designing the business. Bob would be the chief operating officer— the guy in charge of actually running the company day to day.

Bob had always wanted to start a business. He also wanted a partner. He liked the plan. And the chance of going from zero to sixty million in eleven months was tantalizing.

But Bob had qualms. He wasn't sure if he'd be able to get along with his partner. The business plan had flaws in it, such as not paying sufficient attention to the intense competition. And Bob was not truly interested in what he'd actually be doing, which was essentially installing a medical reference library on-line.

Bob's father, a smart businessman, had said, "You'll never be any younger, you don't have kids yet, so this is the time to start a business. If you don't do it now, you'll never do it."

That phrase—"If you don't do it now, you'll never do it"—has lured millions to their doom. It's true that timing is incredibly important. And there *are* opportunities you have to grab or you'll lose them forever. But good timing is rarely the most important thing. Important, yes. Most important, almost never. Thank God, Bob remembered to ask himself what the most important thing really was.

He remembered how he'd felt floundering around on jobs he didn't care about. He'd felt he was dying inside. Certainly there's no chance that life will be wonderful unless you do what you care about. Of course it was hard to be sure. Money is always important. Success makes you feel good, and there's always the chance you can leverage it into something bigger, so that's important. But as he thought about it, it just felt as though the most important thing was doing something he really cared about.

Remembering to ask himself the question, Bob found an answer that felt right, and he let it rule.

So Bob said no to the gold-painted opportunity dangling in front of him and said yes to a smaller job running an experimental entrepreneurship program in rural upstate New York that provided seed money, training, and support for small-town people who wanted to start their own small businesses. He wouldn't make much money, but this work was something Bob truly cared about, and every day would be full of activities he enjoyed, from helping people directly to talking to business leaders about bringing resources into the region.

A good decision? A great decision. A year later Bob was happy. He felt at home. He'd achieved a sense of inner peace—exactly what he'd been wanting—and he felt he could do this work forever. The internet business, Bob learned, never quite got off the ground. Maybe it would've succeeded if Bob had been part of it. Maybe he would've gotten rich. Maybe he would've found another internet start-up to hook up with.

But people who make great choices don't undermine their success by fantasizing about how alternatives would've made them even more successful. That's just a way to make yourself miserable. The gold standard is how good you feel with the choice you've made.

What this means for you

With every big, tough decision you and I make, we begin by staring into the darkness. If everything was clear, there wouldn't be anything to agonize over. That's why it's hard to get through a big decision without an inner emotional struggle, without sweating bullets.

But by asking yourself what the most important thing is, by trusting the answer you find, and by letting your answer have a huge impact on what decision you make, you're giving yourself your best shot at happiness.

Just ask someone with a story of regret to tell. "If only I'd . . ."

"So why didn't you?" you ask. Listen to their answer. It will be all about how they neglected what was most important to them.

If it doesn't just jump out at you

You might say, "But how will I recognize this *most important thing* when I see it?" Good question. You might wonder if looking for the most important thing isn't a recipe for endless delay.

But it's a straightforward law to apply. If you remember to ask yourself what the most important thing is—and if you refuse to accept anyone offering you an off-the-rack answer to this deeply personal question—you'll do just fine. You win when you ask the question, not when you wait until you find the perfect answer.

When I asked people how they knew they had the most important thing, their answers fell into six categories. If the thing you think is the most important falls into any one of these six categories, you've probably nailed it:

- *It's something that will make your life wonderful.* One woman was asked for her hand in marriage by a guy who lived on a big ranch in Oklahoma. She'd have money, horses, wide-open spaces. As she put it, "I'd been niggling myself to death with all these little fears, but the fact was that I had a chance at something wonderful. You don't say no to that." Nothing is more important than the chance to make your life wonderful. (As long as it's something wonderful that you really want.)

- *Or it's something that will enable you to take care of your most important responsibility.* This is the Captain Joseph Hazelwood Memorial Reminder. If your supertanker is making its way through a field of icebergs, you'd better be on deck, in command, and ready for whatever happens. People don't usually completely forget their most important responsibilities, but they often make the mistake of putting them on the same level as everything else. Your most important responsibility should weigh a hundred times more heavily on the scale.

- *Or it's something that will make it possible for you to solve your biggest problem.* Many times we're led to a particular decision because we know it will solve *a* problem. One baby boomer embarked on an expensive month-long European tour, putting his contracting business on hold because he was tired and needed a break. But that wasn't his biggest problem. This guy would be retiring before long, and he didn't have any money saved up; his biggest problem was that he needed a nest egg. But he couldn't see beyond his urgent desire to take a vacation. If only he'd said, "I'm burnt out, but is that my biggest problem when I look at my life as a whole?" Nothing is more important than solving what is really your biggest problem.

- *Or it's something that will address one huge, stubborn fact you've been refusing to accept.* A woman was trying to decide whether to stay in a mediocre marriage to a couch potato. He was a miserable lump of a guy. She'd spent twenty years waiting and hoping for him to change. The fact was that he could never change, nor did he want to. Once she accepted this, the decision to leave came easily. What's more important than coming to grips with reality?

- *Or it's something that fits who you really are.* A thirty-five-year-old woman with a high-powered job on Wall Street had been struggling with the issue of whether or not to have kids. When her younger sisters and her best friends from college all became parents within a three-year period, she started to hit the baby-panic button. "Why do you want to have kids?" she was asked. "Because I'm thirty-five and everyone I know has kids and if I wait much longer, it'll be too late," she answered. This was a good psychological explanation for her panic, but what was the most important thing here? When asked to dig deep, this woman admitted that she was impatient, insensitive, and deeply uninterested in children. The most important thing was for her to accept who she really was. Once she understood the kind of temperament needed to raise a child, she recognized why the best decision for her was not to have a baby. What's more important than being true to who you really are?

- *Or it's something that will encapsulate what is truly the meaning of your life.* What's more important than the meaning of your life? If you make decisions that ignore why you feel you've been placed on this earth, you will eventually feel you have a track record of bad decisions, but if you make every decision with awareness of your life's meaning, you will make great decisions.

Staying true to the meaning of your life is the most important of all most important things. But sometimes you don't realize what you have until you come close to losing it.

When the future of a man and a nation were at stake

This is a story about James Farmer, one of the great civil rights leaders and head of the Congress of Racial Equality during the Civil Rights Movement in the 1960s. Farmer almost made a terrible decision he would've regretted for the rest of his life. Fortunately, at the very last moment, a young woman reminded Farmer of what was for him the most important thing.

It was the time of the Freedom Riders. They were working their way down to the heart of the deep South. They rode buses and attempted to integrate bus stations and lunch counters in the bastion of die-hard resistance. Farmer was both orchestrating and taking part in these Freedom Rides.

At the same time, Farmer's father was dying of cancer. When Farmer told his father of their itinerary his father said, speaking from long experience, "Well, you might make it through the Carolinas. You might even make it through Georgia. But you'll probably be killed in Alabama, and if they don't kill you there, they'll kill you for sure in Mississippi." The old man felt he was watching his son go off to die as he lay dying himself.

Farmer began his journey with the Freedom Riders. Just as the riders were about to enter Alabama, his father died. It was no accident, Farmer believed. He was sure his father died in an attempt to save his son's life, hoping that at that dangerous moment Farmer would leave the riders to go to his funeral. And Farmer did.

But what next? A white Freedom Rider on the bus Farmer would have been on was almost killed. Now the riders were about to leave Montgomery, Alabama, and go to Jackson, Mississippi.

Farmer said he would not join the riders for the last leg of the trip into Mississippi. He gave as his reasons the fact that mail was piling up in their home office, that he was needed to handle press inquiries, that with his father's death another death in his family would be too much.

But, as he admitted later, those were all excuses. The real reason was that he was understandably afraid. Farmer went down to the bus station to say good-bye to the riders. As he shook hands with a young woman who was a CORE member, she looked at him and said, "Please come with us."

The look on her face and the passion in her voice turned Farmer around, and he got on the bus to join this last, most historic leg of the Freedom Rides.

He was attacked. He was thrown in jail. But he wasn't killed. And he found his place in history.

Let's understand why this was a good decision. Pay attention—this is important. Was it good because Farmer turned out to be lucky and he wasn't killed? No. Luck, good or bad, is not what determines the quality of a decision.

This was a good decision because at the very last moment, just before it was too late, Farmer remembered the most important thing. This was still the beginning of a long and landmark struggle. Not going would have kept Farmer from the winds of change sweeping the country. Not going would've been tantamount to resigning from the movement.

Martin Luther King Jr. had a dream for all Americans. James Farmer had a personal dream as well. And this dream would've been destroyed if he'd refused to take part in a great and defining moment. Accepting a risk of death was reasonable when doing so gave his life the meaning he'd been searching for.

The "most important" checklist

The lesson in James Farmer's story lies in how easy it is to lose sight of the most important thing. The best insurance against this is always to stop, look at why you're making a particular choice, and ask yourself, "Is this the most important thing? Or is there something more important?"

To help you determine whether your choice is based on what's most important, here's a checklist:

- *It's more likely long-term than short-term.* "Where did my life go wrong?" people say sometimes. Usually it's not the result of one horribly bad or stupid decision. Instead, people get to this point by substituting the need of the moment—taking the wrong job for fast money, or marrying the wrong person because they're in a time panic. What was really most important would almost always have been something long-term.

- *It will have more to do with what you want than with what other people want.* When people look back with pride to describe a long series of good decisions, one of the comments that occurs again and again is, "Everyone was telling me to . . . , but I listened to myself and . . ." The wisdom and needs of others are important and should never be ignored, but when asking yourself what's the most important thing, your priority should be to listen to yourself.

- *It will more likely be connected to your hopes than your fears.* People most often forget the good things they'll get from a decision. When there's a tree, a ladder, and an apple, there are a lot of ways things can go wrong, but it's usually better to climb up and get the apple rather than to leave it and congratulate yourself for not having fallen. You haven't really asked yourself what's the most important thing if you haven't truly thought about the good things that can come from your choices.

So let's add this all up:

**The most important thing will most often have to do with what
you want for yourself based on your hopes and dreams for the
long term.**

How do you focus on the most important thing?

Let's say you're one smart cookie and, like James Farmer, you remember to think about what's most important as you face a tough
decision. And you see it, too. It hangs there, shining in front of
you. "Whatever happens, don't screw up this marriage." Or
"You've been working your whole life for this—don't walk away
from it now." Or whatever is most important.

What do you do with this priceless knowledge?

You let it rule.

It's as simple as that. We all have a mass—or a mess—of priorities we're struggling to sort out. There are always many things that
are important to us. But do you want to make great choices? Then
give the one most important thing *more weight than all your other priorities combined.*

I'm saying something radical. This is one of the deepest secrets
of people who make great choices. They're ruthless about throwing out *all* of their other priorities to make room for their most
important priority. People who make bad choices just don't seem
to get it. They work so hard to fit in all their priorities, and yet the
bad decisions keep on coming.

---

*When it comes to focusing on the most important thing, be ready, if
necessary, to dump all the other priorities weighing on you. That's the
beauty of this law. You don't have to be the master of everything. You
just have to find the one most important thing; focus on that, and you
won't go wrong.*

Law #2

Don't Decide Until You're Ready

Why not give yourself more time?

T HE temptation, when you're facing a tough decision, is to jump in and just get it over with. This is called acting on impulse. But people who make great decisions understand that you never, ever make a decision until you're ready. Even when you sense what's best for you to do, don't do it until you're sure you're ready.

Heather, who had spent the last three years launching a much-talked-about TV production company, walked me through the time line of her decision-making process. She told me confidently, "I knew ten years ago that at some point I'd quit my job and go off on my own. But I spent seven years sitting with that, gathering information, building up my self-confidence. Let me show you something."

She went to her desk and took out a personal diary with a lock on it, the kind you'd expect a fifteen-year-old girl with a ponytail to have. She flipped through pages near the beginning of the diary until she found the passage she was looking for. Heather glanced up at me. "This is almost exactly ten years ago that I wrote this," she said, before reading aloud, "'This job sucks. But I think any job would suck. I'm just not made to work for other people. I hate taking orders. I like to do things my own way. So I guess that's it. I'm going to have to go start my own business and be my own boss.'"

She closed the diary and added, "I'd thought back then that I'd made a decision. But I hadn't. I just had a hunch. It took me a long time to be ready to turn that hunch into a bona fide decision."

The point is that we should decide only when we're ready. Readiness is the key, not speed. You can make a great decision incredibly quickly if you're ready. Heather waited to act on her decision because she wasn't ready. Stories of people who decide quickly confuse the rest of us when it comes to the issue of readiness. You may be ready quickly. Or you may need time to get ready. It's readiness, though, not speed, that confirms your decision.

So as you think about making the next big decision in your life, give yourself all the permission in the world to wait until you're ready before you make your decision. And that means taking your time—not signing anything, not committing to anything, not burning your bridges, not doing anything that will start you down a road until you're ready to go down that road.

Readiness is key

Right now, your best decision might be to make no decision. Not yet anyway.

If you're feeling the way a lot of people feel facing a big decision, your gut is probably churning inside. The sense of pressure, even panic, can get pretty intense. You don't know what to do, but you have this overwhelming feeling that you have to do *something*. What you've got, my friend, is *decision panic*. There are two ways you can go that are bad. One is to stew and suffer. The other is to act impulsively. Lots of times we do both: first we stew and suffer; then when we get sick of it, we act on impulse.

The pressure to make a decision can come from anywhere. A job offer that lands on your desk. Seeing how much money your brother-in-law is making. A threat from the person you've been living with to leave if certain problems in the relationship aren't dealt with. You feel you have to decide now. But your head's a million miles away from making this decision. You're preoccupied, distracted. You haven't begun to think about what you need to think about. You're not ready to decide.

If you want to be a great decision maker, you will never decide just because you feel pressure to decide. You're in charge of what you do and when you do it, and you decide when you're ready.

How do you know when you're ready? Let's see.

Matt and Vicki

It had been a perfect situation. Matt had grown up in South Boston with his best friend, Doug. They'd gone to college together, and once they started work they continued to be best buddies. As if that wasn't good enough, when Matt married Vicki, she introduced Doug to a woman she worked with named Ally. Eventually Ally and Doug got married, and Ally and Vicki became close friends. These were two couples who did everything together and were blissfully happy. They wanted their children to grow up together.

Then a monkey wrench was thrown in the works. The ad agency Doug worked for was bought by a Los Angeles agency, and he was offered a huge job promotion with that new agency. But he'd have to move to L.A.; the Boston office was closed. Doug did everything he could to find a good ad job in Boston, but there were none, and L.A. was the offer of a lifetime—making big money working for one of the hottest agencies in the country.

All four of them were inconsolable at the thought of losing each other. So Matt and Vicki promised Doug and Ally that they'd move heaven and earth to find a way to move to L.A. themselves. And indeed as soon as the dust cleared they did everything they could to check out job possibilities and housing in and around L.A. That's when difficulties arose. Matt worked for the mayor. It was an important political job, though it didn't pay much, and Matt found that it would be very hard to transfer the career he'd built to L.A.

Matt and Vicki felt this terrible sense of pressure. They flew out to L.A. to look at houses and realized they wouldn't be able to afford to live anywhere near Doug and Ally's neighborhood. This spurred Vicki to see if she could dig up a good job in L.A. that might make the whole plan work. As a preschool teacher, she could find jobs but not the kind of money that made any difference.

Matt talked about making a career change, although it meant going down a rung on the ladder. There were many decisions ahead if they were going to make this work. But it wasn't working.

A couple of years later Matt saw that they'd been in danger without realizing it. Pushing themselves to decide had meant pushing themselves to do things outside their comfort zone. Matt could very easily have ended up with his career in the toilet, broke, and with resentments that might have damaged his precious friendship, maybe his own marriage.

Vicki saved him. After a grueling weekend of talking about how to make it all work out Vicki had said, "Wait a minute. Where's the fire? We both want this to happen, but why the rush? Who said we have to decide this now? Why not give ourselves time to see how it all works out with them there and us here?"

You're ready when you can see

The key lies in what Vicki said: *"Give ourselves time to see."* That's the difference between being ready and not being ready. When you're not ready, you haven't given yourself time to see what you need in order to feel comfortable going forward with the decision. When you see, you're ready. Ultimately it's not a question of time itself. It's a question of time to see.

To see what? Whatever you need to see. Maybe you need to see how you feel. Or how certain events play out. Or what some of your options are. Or to develop new options.

How much time does all this take? Giving yourself time to feel ready isn't wasting time as long as you keep making discoveries. Give yourself time to see, and as long as you keep seeing things that add to the picture, you're not wasting your time.

Of course it's comforting to know you can take the pressure off, but you can get more. By just not deciding until you're ready you get a powerful boost into the ranks of great decision makers.

A dirty little secret

People who make great decisions have a dirty little secret. They make decisions that now and then turn out badly. They make choices that they later see were mistakes. More than you might think. There's no way around this. You can't always make a perfect call on choices that are fraught with uncertainty. In fact, people who make great decisions are at greater risk of making imperfect decisions than the rest of us, and that's for two reasons.

Their ability to make good decisions means they tend to be given the responsibility for making many decisions. If you make many decisions, you'll have your share of boo-boos. Just ask Peter Lynch of Fidelity's Magellan fame. He will freely admit, as he does in his book *One Up on Wall Street,* that he's made plenty of bad decisions in buying and selling stocks. And yet he's a proven great decision maker. He's made so many decisions that he's had a chance for his good decisions to vastly outweigh his bad ones.

Second, the ability of great decision makers means that sooner or later they will have the opportunity to get in on really interesting decisions, and that's just where you run the greatest risk of screwing up. In all of human history, for example, every village has had its wise women. The word would get out. "This gal gives good advice." As a sign of respect, she'd be brought into more and more difficult decisions. The harder the decisions she'd be faced with, the more likely she was to make mistakes. But so what? That's a hallmark of someone who makes great choices. He or she gets in on the really big decisions.

So think about this for a moment. You and I aren't safe from making our share of bad decisions. And the more good decisions we make, the more our risk of making bad decisions increases. But there's one thing we can do to increase immediately the percentage of decisions we make that turn out great: make fewer *unnecessary* bad decisions.

And there's no simpler, faster, more powerful way to cut down on your bad decisions than by never deciding before you're ready. You can make better decisions on average *without actually making better decisions.* Just cut down on bad decisions and your batting average will shoot up.

And the quickest way to cut down on bad decisions is to cut down on *rushed* decisions. Never decide before you're ready, and you'll immediately jump into the A division.

Taking time doesn't always mean taking *time*

It's not about time. Taking a long time to decide is not necessarily prudent. Deciding quickly, sometimes even immediately, is not necessarily impulsive.

Law enforcement officers, particularly when they're members of SWAT teams and other special tactics squads, get training in urban ambush situations. They'll walk through a specially designed maze of streets and buildings, and figures will pop up in windows and doorways. The trainee will have a split second to shoot the figure of a bad guy before he himself is shot. But not all of the pop-up figures are bad guys. Some look bad but have no weapon. Some look innocent but carry something that looks like a weapon, and yet it isn't. Then again the figure of what seems like a mother and baby might turn out to be a woman with an Uzi.

This clearly shows the difference between acting on impulse and acting quickly but with due deliberation. If you're a cop in a real urban setting, people may startle you and even scare you, but if they're not threats you can't shoot them. If they are threats, you can't fail to shoot them. Either way, you have to take that extra measure of care to look and think and evaluate before you're ready to make your split-second decision.

You just have to *see.* As long as you do that, you might need only a second.

What it means to be ready

You avoid impulsiveness by refusing to act until you're ready. How do you *get* ready? You ask yourself what you need. Not what other people need, what you truly need to feel safe and smart and hopeful. Whatever that is.

Have you got that? Then you're ready.

Not deciding until you're ready applies everywhere. Let's take a seemingly trivial example. You're walking down the streets of the city, you turn a corner, and suddenly there it is, your own moment of extreme danger. It's a bakery. A new one. One you'd heard about—you just hadn't expected to come across it now. The smells threaten to grab you and drag you inside.

How do you turn this from a moment where you act on impulse to a moment where you act thoughtfully?

Just like the cop, you give yourself a moment to see what you need. Because it's always you, not the danger or the opportunity of the moment, who should be in charge. Are you on a diet? How much were you planning to eat that day anyway; were you going out for dinner that night? Are you going to come back this way again? Can you walk in and trust yourself to buy just one thing?

You're ready to decide to go in when you know what you need to feel safe, smart, and hopeful about going in.

Regret-proofing your life

Even if it literally takes you no more than fifteen seconds, you're not acting on impulse if you see the truth and tell yourself the truth about what's really going on and what you really need.

Here's a simple procedure to guarantee you will never act before you're ready. Don't decide until you can say, "Even if I'd spent a lot more time, I'd still have made the same decision."

Think about that. You have it in your power to regret-proof your life. Maybe some of your decisions will turn out to have been mistakes, but you'll never be in the position of saying, "If only I'd taken a minute to think about it . . ."

Let your own experience determine how fast you move. Sanford Weill, decision maker extraordinaire, has worked his way through mergers and management to become head of the financial giant Citigroup. Does he think not deciding until you're ready is the same as going slowly? On the contrary. In fact, Weill says, in the August 10, 1999, edition of the *Wall Street Journal,* to make mergers work you should make decisions faster, not slower, than you normally would. Otherwise a lot of stakeholders get scared and confused. The point is that you can make decisions very quickly and still give them due deliberation.

You've always known, haven't you, that there's something about being ready that makes a big difference to you. Now you have full permission to ask yourself if you're ready before you go forward with any decision. People who make great decisions never decide until they feel completely ready.

Law #3

Look for All the Good Things That Can Happen

What's the best outcome you can expect?

YOU'RE walking along the road and you see something that looks vaguely like an alligator. What do you do? That depends.

Maybe you get too close and it is an alligator and it bites off your arm. Or maybe you'll screw up without even realizing it because you assumed it was an alligator when in fact it was really an expensive piece of luggage filled with hundred-dollar bills.

Okay, it's a wild example, but it makes a wildly important point: you can make a bad decision because what you do leads you to disaster, but you can also make a bad decision because you fail to allow for the possibility of something wonderful happening.

And wonderful things happen all the time. All right, I admit that the roadsides are not strewn with alligator-skin luggage stuffed with money. That's too optimistic even for me. But let's look at what happens in the real world when people act on possibilities. People come to America to find a better life, and most do find a better life. Men and women go out to clubs to find a mate, and they do find mates. People go into therapy to grow and change and solve their problems, and most will grow and change and solve their problems. People invest to make money, and most will make money.

None of these wonderful things would have happened if people had overlooked the possibility that these things *could* happen. When you're looking at an option, don't just ask what's the downside—make sure you identify the upside.

Make your decisions as if you were scared of missing a wonderful outcome on the upside.

Looking for the upside

People forget this all the time. Neil Simon did, and it was perhaps his worst mistake. For all his money Neil Simon would be worth twice what he's worth today if he hadn't sold the rights to *The Odd Couple* for a flat fee when they were turning his play into a television series. He forgot to look for the possibility that the new TV show might be a hit. He never even asked himself how much money it could make if things turned out wonderfully.

Great things happen all the time, and it's an amazingly important truth that's too often forgotten.

Looking for good things is a law designed to remind us of this. As you think about your options, look for the blue sky in each one. Ask yourself, "Okay, if these are my choices, what are the best ways that things can turn out for each one of my choices?"

Let's say you're thinking of changing jobs, plus you have the option of going back to school. Well, you have a lot to think about. But for each job, and for the back-to-school option, ask yourself what the best possible outcome might be. Ask yourself, "For each option, if everything turned out great where would that get me?"

You're in danger if you ignore the upside

When it comes to bad decisions, not looking for something wonderful is a silent killer. When it comes to good decisions, Law #3 is the invisible wind beneath our wings. You say you know good things can happen. But when faced with two options, people constantly forget to give full weight to the good things that might come along with each of those options. Consider's Tom's story.

One summer Friday, people around Tom's office—a world-famous architecture and construction firm—started talking about getting together after work for drinks at a posh hotel cocktail lounge. Through the day casual rumors kept spreading about who would be there, and some interesting names popped up. But a lot of people were also saying it was going to be a waste of time and they wanted to get home. "A bunch of suits getting drunk," one woman said. "Who needs it?"

Tom was totally committed to not going. He was tired. A lot of things hadn't been going his way at work and he was bummed out. He'd lost out on a couple of assignments, and some of what he thought were his best ideas had gotten shot down publicly. "I'm just not up for it," Tom told a friend at work.

But still, those rumors about who would be there kept rumbling. Tom's friend said, "Look, I really can't go because I have to pick my kid up from soccer, and Mary and I have been fighting and if I switch plans on her one more time, it ain't gonna be pretty. But you go. Tell me what happens. It'll probably be nothing, but what the hell."

"Forget it," Tom said. "I'm in a bad mood and the whole thing's probably going to be a waste of time—plus I'm this close to picking a fight with somebody and I don't need that."

Then Tom's friend said what great decision makers typically remember to say. "Look, yeah, it'll probably be a waste of time, but the thing is this: You can walk out if it's just a bunch of people from the office getting drunk. You can walk out if you find you're starting to get ticked off. But they're talking about John and Eddie being there, and those guys are *it* as far as the future of this company's concerned."

Tom's friend made a gesture as if to lay his cards on the table. He leaned forward and said, "The thing is, I think there's a ten-percent chance something really interesting and important is going to be talked about. And the downside is no big deal. You waste a little time. The upside is something huge. What the hell. Be there or be square. I think you should go. Put in a good word for me."

Tom saw the wisdom in this thinking, and it turned out even better than he'd dreamed.

Like all rumors, the rumors about the get-together were distorted but not completely inaccurate. John and Eddie, the two guys who owned the company, had planted the rumor to see who would show up. They were interested in creating a top-down revolution, to let go of a lot of people and change the company's focus. John and Eddie were starting to get tired of designing buildings for other developers. They wanted to develop projects on their own. Have more of a stake in a building, make more money.

One of the people they most wanted to let go was Tom's boss, the guy who'd been shooting Tom's ideas down. He was an old-line, pure architecture type. One of the things John and Eddie wanted to find out was the degree to which Tom was lined up with his boss. Or were Tom's ideas in sync with their own?

A hodgepodge of people drifted into the cocktail lounge. There was a "We're just shooting the breeze" quality to the conversation. But Tom could see that something big was happening. Tom was excited at the direction in which things were moving. He had never wanted to be a guy who designed beautiful buildings. He'd wanted to be a guy who made big buildings happen. And he let John and Eddie know it. This was his shot.

Within a month, Tom's boss was out, the firm's name was changed, and Tom was in charge of launching the development of a major office building in midtown Manhattan.

Tom's decision here was whether to go to a stupid cocktail lounge after work for a round of drinks at which maybe a higher-up would make an appearance. There were a lot of reasons, mostly emotional, not to go.

But if there's a chance that something wonderful will happen, and if you remember to ask whether it might happen, then why not pay a small price in the hope of getting a big return?

Great decision makers, if they see a bag lying around, ask themselves, "What if it's stuffed with goodies? What will it cost me to find out?"

Getting the good stuff

How do you put this law of great expectations into practice? Let's first look at the ordinary way to deal with a decision and then at the better way. You're facing two options. Go to a meeting or don't go to the meeting. Invest in the stock market or keep your money in certificates of deposit. Take that big job overseas or stay home. Go back to school to change careers or stick with where you are now. Go out on that blind date or pass it up.

The ordinary way to make these decisions is to compare your two options and think only about the most likely outcome either way. For Tom this would've meant comparing the probability that going for drinks after work would be a waste of time to the probability that if he went home he could rest and have fun.

This method makes common sense, but it's also terribly misguided *if* one option has a possible wonderful outcome that would shift the way you made your decision, if you paid attention to it and gave it full weight.

So instead think about the ways things might turn out to be more wonderful than you first thought. Compare the *best* outcome of each option. Just when things seem cloudiest, always look for the silver lining.

People think of great decision makers as having a special knack for turning a sow's ear into a silk purse. It's easier than that. People who make great decisions remember to look for the hidden wonderfulness of things. Geniuses find things other people would never find. Great decision makers look for things other people would never think of looking for. You can't choose to be a genius, but you can choose to be a great decision maker.

Great things come in four flavors

How do you look for great outcomes when you don't know what they might be? Here are some hints. When you remember to search for the possibility of wonderfulness, you'll find there are four ways your options might turn out better than you thought.

→ The first way is that *you get more of what you were hoping for* from that option. Half the millionaires running around started out hoping to do well, hoping to make a lot of money, but they never dreamed they'd make as much as they actually did make. Half the people who got out of the rat race and tried to find a way of living that would make them happy ended up not only happy, but happier than they dreamed they'd be. So look for ways your options might deliver more of what you were hoping for than you'd first thought.

→ The second way your options might turn out better than you'd thought is that *you get something from them that you never imagined you'd get.* Not more than what you were looking for but a different kind of thing from what you were looking for. You thought of saying no to a blind date, but then you went and although you didn't find the love of your life, you met someone who knew about a great job opportunity that you ended up going for. It's called serendipity. This world, in fact, is dripping with serendipity the way a dowager is dripping with diamonds on opening night at the Met. So look for ways your options might deliver unanticipated benefits.

→ The third way things might turn out better than you'd thought is that *the outcome you were looking for might be much more likely to happen than you'd realized.* For example, your back had been hurting, and you'd wondered about seeing a physical therapist. There was the expense to worry about and concern about whether the physical therapist would be a dud, and whether all the physical work you'd have to do in order to heal yourself would pay off. But then you realized that you were willing to work and that you would never go with a therapist who didn't come highly recommended. With your being ready for therapy and having a half-decent therapist, how could something good not come out of the experience? So look for ways your options might deliver good outcomes more easily than you first thought.

→ And the fourth way things might turn out better than you'd thought is that *the outcome you were looking for comes with a much smaller price tag than you'd thought.* After all, real bargains are wonderful. Let's say you're twenty-five years old, you have training in computers, and an uncle has just left you fifty thousand dollars. Why not start your own business? Will you probably fail? Yes.

Those are the statistical odds, anyway. But how much would it really cost you? You didn't need the fifty thousand at twenty-five years of age, nor had you been counting on it. You're young enough to have time to make mistakes, and anyway, you'll be using other people's money. *Whatever happens, you'll learn some incredible lessons.* Now add up the cost, and you'll see it's not that much. If you win, you win. If you lose, you still come away with a fifty-thousand-dollar education. So look at ways your options will deliver their benefits more cheaply than you'd first thought.

Practical optimism

Wonderfulness can turn up everywhere and in many different guises. So do this: for every option you're facing, remember this law. Be realistic, but ask yourself what is the best that could happen if you chose that option. Let hardheaded but full-blown optimism have its place at the table. Your choices might then look very different to you.

You're not really under any obligation to uncover all the blue-sky potential in your options. You're using Law #3 properly when you simply remember to ask yourself how things might turn out better than you'd thought.

Overcoming fear of blue skies

This law makes so much sense that the big question is why any of us would ever forget it. Here are the main reasons, and here's what to do about them if they're operating in your case.

→ *Feeling like a naïve idiot.*
Suppose someone you know and trust is starting up a business and looking for investors. He gives you his pitch, and it sounds good. You talk to some friends about it. Friends being the way they are, they may start bringing out their qualms and quibbles. They seem so smart seeking out possible problems that you start feeling like a fool at the thought of going ahead with the deal. They'll probably think you're a fool too if you do go ahead, you think.

This kind of thing happens to us when we start dating someone, when we contemplate a career change, whenever we face a big decision. Helpful friends caution us into a state of discouragement, and we feel stupid not agreeing with them. And so we assassinate the blue sky lurking in our options.

Well, you should check out a friend's investment scheme very carefully. People get creamed all the time when situations like these turn sour. Walk away if you smell a rat. But remember that this is how every billion-dollar enterprise got started. From Microsoft on down, the first investors are always friends and relatives. Don't decline the offer, don't turn your nose up at any opportunity, just because you're afraid to look like a naïve idiot. Optimism that remains after you've checked things out is not naïve.

→ *Fatigue.*

This was Tom's problem, if you remember. He was just too tired to think about what he might get by going out for drinks after work. You have to watch out for fatigue. It creeps in and whispers to you, "Let go, give up, go home, stop trying." Fatigue will say anything to win. Most of all, fatigue will try to discount what you might get from putting out more effort.

So think of your fatigue as a highly partisan, win-at-all-costs adviser who cares nothing about your best interests. If you are truly exhausted, rest first, then decide. But don't ever let your fatigue convince you that impressive rewards from effort aren't there. Why should your being tired mean that there's no upside?

→ *You've been burnt.*

You have to kiss a lot of frogs before you find your prince or princess. But that means kissing a lot of frogs. Pretty soon you begin to feel that there's no prince or princess out there.

Big mistake. Think about the stock market. There are two ways to screw up on Wall Street. One is to lose money. The other is to fail to make money when everyone else is making money. This is much more devastating. If you don't go for the gains that outweigh the losses, then the losses will swamp you.

In the same way, if all you do is focus on the ways you've been burnt, you'll end up in what I call the *do-nothing trap*. You won't put out effort because you're afraid something bad will happen, but nothing good will happen either. The less effort you put out, the fewer good things will happen and the more convinced you become that there's no gold in them thar hills. You've got a one-way ticket to Palookaville.

What does being burnt tell you? It tells you there are potholes on the road. Okay, avoid potholes. But don't avoid roads. Think about where you want to go and the best way to get there, then worry about hitting potholes. But don't let the potholes keep you from taking the trip.

What is so hard about checking out the possibility that some of your options may turn out great? You don't have to do anything special. You just have to get past the discouragement, fatigue, and fear of seeming naïve that have prevented you from seeing the upside. Once you see it, you'll see the smartest way to decide. We make decisions to make things wonderful. So make the decision that actually offers the most wonderful outcomes. Why settle for less?

Law #4

Choose It or Lose It

What big decision are you not making now?

A N important difference between good and bad decision makers lies in the kinds of things they make decisions about. It's
not that good decision makers are better at hitting the bull's-eye, but
they're better at coming up with bull's-eyes to hit in the first place.

Almost everyone wrestles with big decisions in life. If you ask
someone what he's working on in his life now, he'll probably tell
you about some decision that's been dropped on his in-basket by
circumstances. He got a job offer. The person he's been seeing gave
him an ultimatum on getting married. A stock she put a lot of
money into suddenly dropped in price.

But suppose he tells you about a decision he wants to make that
his boss and his spouse and time itself *aren't* foisting on him. That
guy is probably one fine decision maker.

**We all eventually make the decisions we have to make. It's the
great decision makers who take on the decisions they don't have
to make.**

Look on your back burner

Think about what this law says. There on the front burner are all
the decisions that are being forced on you. Fine. But there on the

back burner are decisions you could make about important issues in your life. Make one of those big, tough, *deferrable* decisions, and you'll become a better decision maker.

Victor's story

You wouldn't say Victor looked like a great decision maker, unless your idea of making great decisions is eating a lot of lo mein and cheesecake. But he was. His parents had worked in the costume jewelry manufacturing business in Rhode Island. His mother had been an ace bookkeeper and his father a reputable toolmaker in costume jewelry manufacturing. But they had just worked for wages; Vic wanted his own business.

That's what he did. He worked. He saved. Eventually, with a ton of debt, Vic bought a small factory. And with his manufacturing know-how the business thrived and grew. Like all small businessmen, he spent his time putting out fires and working on the next project. But in the back of his mind he was worried about foreign competition. Other guys in the business worried too, but the story they told was about how they'd win by doing things the way they'd always done them. Just keep on with high-quality, low-cost methods and you'll be fine, they said.

This is the way most of us deal with nagging worries at the back of our mind. Whatever we've done to get us as far as we've gotten, we think we'll be fine if we keep on doing those things.

Vic didn't have to do anything besides keep on keeping on. His accountant told him, "If I had books like yours, I wouldn't do a damn thing differently." But Vic knew he was vulnerable. As easy as it was to do nothing, there were a ton of smart businessmen in countries where workers made ten cents a day. How could he ignore that threat?

At first, Vic didn't know where to start. All he knew was manufacturing, the world didn't need another jewelry importer, and he wasn't a marketing guy. He asked some of his customers a seemingly crazy question: "Why do you buy from me when you could go overseas?" They told him hair-raising stories about low-quality, unreliable manufacturing.

That was Vic's clue. He started a new business as an outsourcing middleman. You want to manufacture abroad? Call Vic, and he'll check things out. At first he worked as a consultant, but this was just a way for him to get paid to learn the lay of the land. Once he made enough contacts, and developed a reputation abroad as the guy you couldn't put one over on when it came to manufacturing jewelry, he started taking on long-term contracts.

It was a neat business. One guy made the pie, another sold it, but Vic always got a piece of the pie. And he kept his factory back in Rhode Island the whole time. Vic became a force to be reckoned with in the international costume jewelry business.

Close the barn door before the horse escapes

Everyone had thought Vic was wasting his time. That's the way we often feel when we make decisions we don't have to make. Who needs all that work and trouble?

Just remember: it's the decisions you don't have to make that save you from a world of disaster and bring you a world of wonderful things.

The saddest stories I know are of those people who thought they had the luxury of not choosing, and therefore they never made a decision that they found easy to avoid. And yet there were decisions to make.

Erica on ice

Erica had spent her twenties in relationships with guys who weren't right for her. When she was twenty-nine she met Brian. He was rugged, warm, and sincere. Strong but not macho. A former professional hockey player, he was trying to get some direction in his life, but he seemed like a winner.

They fell in love and moved in together. Within a couple of years it was clear to Erica that Brian had problems. He wanted to do something that would give him the prestige and emotional highs of hockey. But it was hard for him to find anything like that. He spent a lot of time sitting around the house watching television and drinking beer. He got on Erica's case for the way she did things. The worse he felt about himself, the more he picked on her, and the worse she felt about him.

But Brian was still a good guy and had promise, Erica thought. Most of the time they got along okay. He told her that he planned to marry her and that they would have kids together. So she decided to stay with him.

Drifting is the default option of people who make bad choices. It is a choice. Every day that Erica stayed with Brian was a day when she was making a major decision without even realizing it. She was deciding to stay childless when she wanted children. She was deciding to stay with a man who made her resentful and didn't meet her needs when she wanted a man who could pull his weight.

But these decisions were invisible to her. Inside, Erica, like anyone who's violating this law, was experiencing a kaleidoscope of feelings alternating between hope and worry, despair and numbness. She was, in other words, riding the misery train to nowhere.

For someone who's drifting, the excuse is always the same: things aren't so bad.

Waiters need not apply

People who make great choices don't act on impulse. But when they have all the evidence they're going to get and when they've examined all the angles they can examine, they go ahead and make the damn decision.

People who make good choices *make choices*. They don't wait for "events to play out." They don't say, "I'll know what I want to do when I see what I've done." They don't say, "Eventually the right decision will come to me." They don't use any excuse for procrastinating. They understand that you either *choose it or lose it*.

My father's tragedy

Everyone acts when there's a knife to his throat. But will you act *before* things get so bad that you have *to* act? When we act in reaction to crises and difficulties that reach dramatic levels, we make poor choices, to say nothing of the fact that it's a poor choice to wait that long in the first place.

Failure to observe this law ruined my father's life. Born in 1910, my father was on track to finish college in 1932. Then came the Depression. He didn't have enough money to finish his last year of college, but in those days three years of engineering study was pretty darn good.

The Depression years turned into the war years. After World War II he worked as an engineer, but he never got the kind of job his talents should've earned him. On a couple of occasions he lied about having a degree, but because he did defense work and had to have security clearances, he was found out and fired.

My father had good options all along. He could've been a technician. He could've gone back to school. He could've gotten out of engineering altogether. But he made none of those choices.

The older he got, the harder it got. In his thirties he got married and had a child, and it seemed silly to him to go back to school. In his forties, he looked back on his thirties as a great period to have gone back to school. As he got older, he was at greater risk of being fired and going back to school seemed that much more ridiculous.

I remember his last engineering job. I remember the tiny gray metal desk in the tiny office. It was a very small manufacturing facility. His boss was a "real" engineer and a horrible guy. My father was his assistant, a kind of semi-high-tech gofer. It was deeply humiliating, and it was the last in a chain of events that turned my father into a broken man.

This chain of events began with my father's avoiding a decision—what to do about his lack of an engineering degree. Many of life's catastrophes are the result of some deferred decision. It's not convenient to make the decision. But deciding will save you from the erosion of possibilities that comes when you fail to realize that you have to choose it or lose it.

This truly does mean that most of us are one or two decisions away from something wonderful. Not just a turning from the road to nowhere but a new start, on a better road that leads us somewhere we want to go.

How do you do this? Here's what people who make great decisions do. They remember to ask one question:

THE CHOOSE-IT-OR-LOSE-IT QUESTION

What problems, needs, or situations am I not paying attention to that I must make a decision about?

People who understood this law have saved America from disaster over the past fifteen years. Corporate America was in trouble and Japan was killing us. Everyone was saying that it was the end of American financial superiority and independence.

It was corporate restructuring that saved us. Now, each little individual act of corporate restructuring was a painful decision that could've been deferred for much longer, because it had already been deferred for a long time. Like Erica's drifting with Brian. Like my father's drifting with an unfinished degree. In every case the easiest thing was to do nothing, and slowly watch it all drift away. But by finally tackling the deferred decision to make American business lean and mean, to cut costs and create reinvestable profits, we created an unprecedented epic of prosperity.

Focus your attention and energy on the decisions you've been avoiding. The best decision you'll ever make is probably one you've been putting off.

Law #5

Base Your Decision on Self-Acceptance

Does your decision fit the real you?

O UR destinies, for good or ill, are determined by whether or not we have a rendezvous with self-acceptance. This law says you don't have to change who you are to make a good decision. If you accept who you really are—imperfect as you may be— you will make great decisions.

We make our lives hard by refusing to accept what we know is true about who we really are. The way good decisions and self-acceptance go hand in hand comes up everywhere. Our careers are particularly vulnerable. For instance, consider two people, both financial types, both wanting to get ahead.

One accepts who she is and decides to build on her strengths. She decides to let her ability with numbers take her as far as it can. If there are other things she needs to learn, she'll pick them up along the way. She goes far.

The other hates who he is, believing he should be good with people and that he can make himself be good with people. He decides to go into sales; essentially he tries to build a career on self-rejection. He goes nowhere.

You've probably seen this yourself. A friend announces she's getting married, but the guy's broke! You know your friend runs on money the way a Ferrari runs on gas. She grew up with it. She likes it. She needs it. Maybe that's not something to be proud of, but it's oh-so-real. You just know your friend is stepping into a bad decision and screwing up her future. Why? Because it's hard for her to accept the reality that for her there's no romance without finance.

How to use self-acceptance to make good decisions

You'd be amazed at how powerful this law of self-acceptance is. People who make great decisions intuitively understand that you can change your life if you accept the things you can't change about yourself. Horizons open when you accept yourself. Disasters are avoided.

People whose decisions keep turning out badly are often using a decision to try to be someone they're not. They're either trying to reinvent themselves or they're simply ignoring tough truths about themselves.

All this law requires is being able to look in the mirror and accept some tough truths about yourself. Whatever big decision you're facing, do this: Go to the mirror, look yourself in the eye, and ask, "What about me needs to be true for this decision to work out? Are these things in fact true?"

Suppose you find that there's a mismatch between what is true about you and what you need to be true for your decision to be a success. Then you're headed for disaster. It's like buying a bathing suit. You can think you're skinnier than you really are and make a bad bathing-suit-buying decision, or you can accept the lumps and bulges in your shape and buy a bathing suit that actually makes you look good.

Jennifer's story, as you'll see, makes it clear that every decision starts as a fork in the road. Will we start with self-delusion and take the path to disaster? Or will we start with a clear-eyed gaze at the truth about ourselves, even if the truth isn't flattering, and take the path to success?

A real story of success in Hollywood

Jennifer graduated from Brandeis with dreams of being a movie-maker. A *film*maker, like Steven Spielberg. She was an economics major in college, but she took all of the film courses she could. And she hated them. She thought she hated them because she was, like, *real*. You know, a practical filmmaker, not one of these talky, arty types.

After college she bummed around a bit. Just to have fun, but also because she was a little afraid of going to Hollywood and finally bumping into her destiny. She didn't trust herself to make the best decisions when she got there. Within a couple of years, though, she grew up a little, got to Hollywood, and learned that one of the fastest ways to get paid for being on a movie set was to become a script supervisor. If you've ever seen a movie about making movies, she's the woman (it's usually a woman) with a clipboard and stopwatch who keeps track of who does what when.

She hung around with people who were developing scripts, people who wanted to make movies the way she'd talked about wanting to make movies. But she realized it was horrible. Here in the place where dreams can come true she hated the people who were doing what she wanted to do. She hated their empty talk. She hated the people who were flailing around searching for that supercommercial concept. She hated the alternative-film-type people who were grasping for the perfect anticommercial concept.

She was discovering that her dream wasn't fun for her. It was disturbing to her to see the way her wanna-be moviemaker pals all seemed deeply clueless about making money.

Jennifer got a job working as an assistant producer on a low-budget film, and she learned something so startling and so hard to accept about herself that she spent years running away from it. She liked money, she liked business, and she liked the part of Hollywood that was a business. That was the part that fit who she really was.

When she looked into the mirror of truth, she saw that the only part of her that wanted to be a film "artist" was the part that wanted to *say*, "I'm a film artist." To see the truth, she went back to the fact that she'd been an economics major in college. Now she saw who she really was.

She'd thought that made her a boring, empty person, and that had been hard for her to accept. So with a huge gulp she faced the truth about how she worked. Real moviemakers wanted to make movies, and they cared about the things that went into making movies. She wanted to make money, and she cared about the things that went into making money. She dumped her artist dreams before she'd have to suffer for them and went to work for a talent agency. Her old self would've said this decision was just about money. Her real self said, "This is where the action is. This is fun. This is real. This is *me*." It felt much better to accept herself for who she really was than to sell her true self down the river so she could tell people she was a filmmaker.

And so one more successful decision maker is born.

When it's hard to face the real you

Any lack of self-acceptance will result in bad decisions. Take Ann. She hated her marriage, but she couldn't leave it because she couldn't accept the truth about herself. The image she *wanted* to be true was that she'd found her soul mate and so she should be happy. And in some ways Ivan was her soul mate. He was as passionate about politics as she was, he was a kind man, and he was an excellent father to their children.

There was just one problem. They weren't physically compatible. Sensuality meant everything to Ann—it's what she really cared about—but Ivan did nothing for her sexually. He was also a bit shorter than she was, a fact Ann hated to admit was important to her. Feminists were not supposed to be turned on by big, strong men and turned off by short, dumpling men. They were supposed to be turned on by the man's mind. Ann desperately wanted to be the way she thought she was supposed to be and not the way she really was.

Ultimately, of course, you can run but you can't hide. Ann fell into brief, guilt-shrouded affairs with the kinds of guys who did something for her sexually. Her marriage to Ivan descended into a nightmare of bitterness. For no reason as far as Ivan could tell, Ann began acting as if she couldn't stand him. But every day she made the terrible decision to stay and drag out their pain because she couldn't accept herself.

"A person like me just *can't* be the way I am," she said when I confronted her with the truth about her sexuality. But you can *only* be the way you are. Ann wasted far too much time in a marriage to a good man who wasn't right for her. She realized that the "you" you want to be can never make the "you" you really are happy.

Finally Ann accepted something we all need to realize:

There is no bad news about who you really are.

The bad news comes when you refuse to accept who you are and make decisions that are terribly wrong for you.

One thing at a time

We're often led into violating this law—*Base your decisions on self-acceptance*—because we think that basing a decision on who we'd like to be will help us *become* who we'd like to be. But this is the same as saying, "Since I'd like to be someone who knows how to swim, I'll just jump off the end of the dock like a real swimmer and that will help me become a real swimmer." No, it will help you become a drowning victim.

Make a decision to change yourself if you want to and if it makes sense. Make all your other decisions based on who you really are, right now. Just keep the two very separate.

Trying to be brave

Bill didn't follow this law. He was a brilliant, successful computer consultant whose work life consisted of being led from one challenging technical assignment to another, but Bill couldn't stand the thought that every guy who hired him was richer, braver, and less intelligent than he was. He wanted to be a brave, risk-taking swashbuckler like the guys he worked for. "I'm not brave, but I want to be brave, and maybe the only way to become brave is to do brave things," he told me. Oh boy, I thought. I could just smell the bad decisions coming.

As someone who hated and feared risk but hated himself for hating and fearing risk, Bill careened wildly between taking on gigantic risks and being paralyzed into inaction. He took on jobs he couldn't handle, failed publicly, and damaged his reputation as a problem solver.

I said, "Just because you feel you should be like the guys you work for doesn't mean you are like them." To test this radical thought, Bill made a deal with me. He'd stay a consultant while trying to change who he was. If he managed to discover his inner daredevil, fine, he could embrace entrepreneurship. If not, he'd know the kinds of bad decisions he'd be better off avoiding.

There was no inner daredevil. If there is, we usually know about it. Bill briefly mourned the death of his alter ego. He was shocked to discover how much fun his life was once he let go of the stress that came from thinking he should seek out risk. He'd thought he'd end up seeing himself as a smaller man. Instead he ended up feeling like a freer man.

This is always the exciting result of basing your decisions on self-acceptance. It's hard to do at first. It feels wonderful later.

The next step

Think about three truths that are hard for you to accept about yourself. Three self-truths that might make a mockery of one of the options you're considering. We've all got things like this hidden in the cupboards of our minds. I'm talking about things like:

- "I'm basically lazy." Does it make sense then for you to march down that career path that only works for eighty-hour-a-week types, even though that career path was what you thought you wanted?

- "I'd like to think of myself as a nice guy, but I really need to be in control. I'm more comfortable ordering people around than wondering if they like me." Does it make sense then for you to take a job at the social service agency that runs on collective decision making and collegiality, even though you love to help people?

- "I hate complications and I hate worry." Does it make sense then for you to get involved with risky, go-go investments even though you want to make money?

You don't need to go into psychoanalysis to discover your own truths. These are the lumps and bumps of your personality that you already know about. That's the whole point of basing your decisions on self-acceptance. You don't have to discover these things, you just have to accept them.

Then say to yourself, "Suppose I accept the fact that these things are true about me. I don't want them to be true, but they are true. Is this decision I'm thinking of making going to work, given that these things are true about me?"

Answer this question honestly. If you're having trouble accepting yourself for who you really are, accept this *fact:* If you make a decision at odds with who you really are, you'll end up putting all your energy into propping up a structure that never should have been built.

If you're a short, skinny guy, why suffer trying to play professional basketball when you can be a happy jockey? Smart decision makers accept themselves and have a deep trust that there is a place in the world for who they are *as* they are.

If you accept who you are as the basis for your decision . . . well, you see, that's how imperfect people make great choices. They can trust themselves because they know there won't be buried parts of who they are that will come back to haunt them. By following this law, as you live with your decision, you will have the experience of coming home to yourself.

Perspectives

The Top Ten Biggest Decisions

Tₕᵢₛ book is not a cookbook with all the answers on how to change your life. It's about giving you the tools for you not only to make a great decision but to feel like someone who is going to make a great decision no matter what's thrown at you.

No matter how confused you are by a particular decision, no matter how stupid or ignorant you feel about it, you are still the world's leading expert on your life. After practicing psychotherapy for almost twenty-five years I've learned to have a deep respect for people's knowledge of themselves and their lives.

But let's face it—there are certain huge decisions we all face in common. We all have to face the same decisions about work and love and money and health. The specifics are wildly different from one person to another. The deep issues are amazingly similar.

Here are the top ten big decisions we all face, as well as some bits of wisdom and guidance from great decision makers about how to make these decisions so you get what you need.

Remember that the suggestions here are broad. Nothing can substitute for religiously following the thirty laws and thoughtfully applying them to the realities of your life. But this is what people who make great decisions say about the Top Ten Biggest Decisions in life.

1. *Whom to marry, and when*

Men: you should get married sooner than you think. A lot of men wait too long, thinking they have all the time in the world. All the smart men who've been where you are say the same thing—start looking early on for a woman you want to marry, and when you find her, grab her.

Women: you should think about getting married *later* than you probably had in mind. Too many women feel too much pressure too soon. Do yourself and your future partner a favor by taking the pressure off yourself until you know who you are and what you want.

As for whom to marry? Obviously this is an enormously personal decision, but I'm here on bended knees begging you to pay attention to some fantastically important basic principles. Smart people who've been farther down this road than you all say:

- *Marry someone you like.* We all think love is important. But really *liking* someone is even more important.

- *Marry someone who's not crazy.* Why the hell do people violate this principle? Maybe they think crazy is interesting. It isn't. It messes you up, and everyone around you. Don't marry anyone with mental or emotional problems.

- *Marry someone you have fun with.* Fun is the glue of intimacy. It's the rubber on the tires of love. Look, here's a fact: people who have fun together can weather all kinds of storms. People who don't have fun together sink in a drizzle.

- *Marry the smartest, most solid person you can find.* A life with someone where you have to deal with children and money and career issues really is like sailing through a storm. Who do you want to be the cocaptain of your ship—a flake? a baby? No. You want exactly the kind of person you'd want to be the cocaptain of your actual ship if you went through an actual storm. Smart people are winners. Marry a smart person.

- *Marry someone who has the same vision you do for how you'll spend your lives.* You marry a lifestyle as much as you marry a person. How can the marriage be solid if you're always battling over your lifestyle? How can the marriage not be solid if you both want to live the same way?

2. What career to choose

This question is not just for young people. More and more of us are changing careers at different points along the way, and often we're changing more than once. So what should we think about when we're making a career decision?

- *Forget about the money.* Money's important, but with rare exceptions different careers don't really represent that much difference in income for a person of a given level of education. Happiness is having enough money to pay your bills and not worry. More money than that doesn't make you happy. The internet billionaires who did it just for the money aren't happy. The ones who didn't do it for the money—they're happy, but it's not their money that's making them happy.

- *Don't try to impress other people.* Whether we like it or not, we use our career as the ultimate fashion accessory. The answer we give when we're asked "What do you do?" can make us feel better than a two-thousand-dollar suit. But if we choose a career we don't like, we'll never be happy no matter how impressed other people will be. And trust me on this: if what you do makes you feel good, you won't care what other people think.

- *Never choose a career based on trying to be something you're not.* If you try to attain self-improvement via a career choice, you probably won't improve yourself, and you'll almost certainly set yourself up for a lousy career experience. Instead, choose a career the way you'd choose your clothes: pick one that emphasizes your good points and hides your flaws.

- *Look for growth opportunities.* There is more to you than you think. More than other people think. You need a career that will enable you to experience yourself as someone who grows in knowledge, power, skill, experience, maturity. Choose whatever career is right for you, but be very skeptical of careers where thirty years from now you're going to be doing exactly what you're doing today. In other words, don't just look for a career, look for a career path. If you don't choose a career that has lots of open doors, you're going to have to break open doors yourself.

3. Where to live

Your work determines where you live, and then you just find a place not too far away from it. What's the problem?

Well, if there's no problem, why do people agonize before they make this decision? More important, why do people so often suffer after they've made this decision?

Here are some extra, not-so-obvious tips on deciding where to live that people who make great decisions have shared with me.

- *Get the least expensive place you can.* Nothing will mess your life up more than falling in love with a too-expensive home, and then thinking you can find a way to "swing" it. In fact it will suck you dry financially and emotionally. Just look at where the smartest businesspeople live. More often than not their homes are surprisingly modest, and they're usually incredibly modest given their level of wealth. A less expensive house means more money for your retirement or for other things that matter to you.

- *Live as close to a city as you possibly can.* This is controversial. If you absolutely love the country and hate the city, you have to live in the place you love. And of course this doesn't apply to farmers! But in general, the closer to the city you can get, the happier everyone in your family will be. That's because there are more opportunities in cities. More good things for your kids to do. More culture for you. More different ways to make money.

- *Minimize your commuting time.* I see it happen over and over. People live too far from where they work because they think that some distant suburb will be good for the kids. The kids hate it because there's nothing to do there. The parents hate it because they have to spend all their time driving their kids around, whatever time they have left from driving themselves to and from work. Why make yourself miserable? An hour a day cut from your commuting time (that's half an hour each way) is a gift of 250 hours a year. Think of it as just about a free two-week vacation.

• *Never live anywhere that depresses you.* I understand that you would never deliberately move somewhere because it depresses you. But people make what they think are realistic compromises for the sake of some "higher" value. Pleasing your partner, perhaps, or making more money. Then they think they can rise above their depressing surroundings. But it usually doesn't work that way. Depressing surroundings usually get more depressing with time. If you have any choice at all, choose not to be depressed by where you live.

4. Whether and when to have children

If you want to have children, don't agonize over when, because there's no perfect time. Whenever you have them, you'll find a way to make it work. My first child was born when I was twenty-one, which is pretty young for a guy to have a first child. There were a lot of problems, given my being such a kid myself and our not having any money. But there was a youthful connection between me and my children. I had a lot to give when they were teenagers, and—joy of joys—I was only forty-two when my youngest went off to college. My best friend had his first kid twenty years after I did. It's working out great for him too.

And don't agonize over not having children. People who are childless by choice are generally happier than people with children. The time and money and freedom that become available when you don't have kids are a wonderful gift and a great opportunity.

So whatever happens, be happy. Everything else is details.

5. Whether to change jobs

The old ideal is still an ideal: joining a company when you're just starting out and growing your career as the company grows. Hey, it worked for Bill Gates. Do it if you can.

These days most of us can't. Change happens. And if it doesn't happen to you, you may very well need to make it happen. The question is, *when* should you change jobs? Here's when:

- *When you have a bad boss.* There are books about coping with bad bosses. But the best advice is to run for the hills. You can cope with a bad boss, but you can never cope well. Coping with a bad boss is like coping with a ferret in your pants. The very first day you discover that your boss is stupid, incompetent, mean, selfish, destructive, blind, or simply a bad match for you, actively search for a new job and don't stop until you get one. Even if it's a worse job, a worse job with a better boss is better than a better job with a bad boss.

- *When there's no room for advancement.* I'm not necessarily talking about climbing the corporate ladder here. I'm talking much more broadly about your having a sense that the place where you work is a place where you can shine. So don't let yourself stagnate. And you have to look carefully for the signs of stagnation. It can be hidden by your sense that you've grown expert at your job, that you've become indispensable to your department, that you're comfortable with your routine. You should be seeking out a sense of confidence and comfort. But the minute you find it, start looking for a way to move on.

- *When you have an opportunity to work for a good company.* Unless you are actually a turnaround specialist, in which case you'll be paid for your trouble, no job offer is attractive if it's attached to a less-than-healthy company. When companies catch cold, it's the employees who get pneumonia. The rats will desert the sinking ship anyway. Just make sure you're one of the first rats to go.

- *When your job is a source of pain.* Let me define "feeling good" when it comes to your job, because we all understand that while a job shouldn't be purgatory it probably won't always be a picnic either. At the end of the day, ask yourself whether you just had a good day or a bad day. You can't say "in between." Good or bad. That's it. Then on your calendar write down "good" or "bad" for that day. If thirty days go by and there are more "bads" than "goods," then your job does not feel good. It feels bad. It's time to leave. Here's another test. Even if your job feels okay, ask yourself how you'd feel doing it for the rest of your life. If the thought of doing it for a lifetime hurts, change jobs now. People who make good decisions have a lower tolerance for pain on the job than the rest of us. They don't make impulsive decisions as a way of dealing with their pain. But they don't put up with the pain.

- *When you have a chance to learn new skills, alternate lateral and upward moves.* This is a powerful little trick. It's rare that you can get where you want to go by taking a straight line upward. That's only for the lucky few. The rest of us need to do something like the following (and please don't feel you have to carry out this prescription rigidly): Let your next job be a lateral move (no real promotion or big pay hike) to one where you add something valuable to your résumé. This might be a job where you learn new skills or take on different responsibilities. It's not a promotion, but that lateral move should put you in a better position to make an upward move next time. If you focus too narrowly on getting more money or a better title with every new job, you'll lose out on those learning experiences that can skyrocket you ahead later.

- *When the job will be fun, give yourself a pleasure promotion.* Why should money or career advancement be your only reasons for changing jobs? At least once in your life take a job because it's more fun. I call this getting a pleasure promotion. It may not be a better job on paper, but it feels better to do it.

6. Whether to get divorced
I collaborated with Mira Kirshenbaum on the book *Too Good to Leave, Too Bad to Stay: A Step-by-Step Guide to Deciding Whether to Stay In or Get Out of Your Relationship*. If you're wrestling with the question of staying in or getting out of an iffy relationship, that book will give you everything you need. There are thirty-six guidelines. Here's the first: *If it never was very good, it never will be very good.*

7. How much to save and what to invest in
The saving part is clear. If I had to decide whether someone was a good or bad decision maker and I could ask only one question, my one question would be, "Do you save ten percent of your yearly income?" Good decision makers tend to save about this much or more. Poor decision makers tend to save a lot less.

It makes sense. Good decision makers think about the future. Poor decision makers are driven by impulse.

And what to invest in? I've invested my whole life, and I've done very well. As of today I can make a good living as an investor without having to do anything else. But instead of setting myself up as the expert here, let me pull together the expertise of everyday men and women who can look back on decades of good investment decisions.

There are two keys.

The first is consistency. Keep yourself invested. Keep putting new money into your investments. Don't try to time the market. You've got to keep planting if you want your garden to keep growing.

The second key is buying growth stocks. The best way to do this for most people is to buy mutual funds with a good track record of investing in growth stocks. Don't buy stocks yourself unless you have a damned good reason to believe you can do a better job of buying stocks than the manager of a good mutual fund.

8. What to do about a particular health problem
Here are the things that people who make great decisions do about health problems.

First, they go to the best doctor they can find. Not their best friend's doctor. Not the closest doctor. But a doctor who has a solid reputation and who specializes in their problem. And then they listen to that doctor.

They always get a second opinion. No matter how much it costs, no matter how inconvenient, the more serious the health problem, the more valuable the second opinion. And if the first two doctors are wildly at odds, they get a third opinion.

Third, they understand that the patient is the one with the greatest responsibility for his own health care. If you don't actively, even passionately embrace your doctor's suggestions for what you need to do, such as diet and exercise, then you might as well just sign up on the side of your disease.

9. What to do when your kid has a problem

This one might surprise you. It's true that people who make good decisions look for the best specialist if their kid has a serious problem. But they also do something you might not expect.

They assume that their kid is probably okay. People who make bad decisions are constantly saddling their kids with labels and dragging them off to therapists. The one time in ten when this is justified is swamped by the nine times in ten when these parents are making a normal kid feel bad about himself.

This whole book is based on the idea that if you just clear away the garbage you can trust yourself to make great decisions. Parents who label their kids and always look for problems are giving their kids the message that they can't trust themselves. This creates a kid with far bigger problems than whatever it was the parent was trying to deal with in the first place.

Try saying this about your kid: "He may not be all I'd hoped he'd be, and sometimes he's a handful, but he's strong and healthy and he knows what's good for him and he's doing the best he can to find his place in life."

10. How to retire

You retire *to* something, not *from* something. This is a deep insight of people who make great decisions. So if necessary, just keep on working until you come up with a good idea of how you want to spend your retirement years. People who just say, "Let me get the hell out of here," can be as lost and unhappy as teenagers. People who know where they're going and why they're going there have happy retirements.

For that matter, people who know where they're going and why they're going there have happy lives.

Law #6

Look Ahead

How will your decision play out over time?

THIS law marks one of the widest gaps between people who make good choices and people who make more than their share of bad choices. People who make bad choices will often have very plausible-sounding reasons for why their choice is a good one. You can sound awfully smart on your way to making a stupid decision.

But listen for a phrase people who make good choices use over and over. If you come to one of these people for advice and lay out all your clever pros and cons, they'll think for a moment and then say, "Yeah, but how will it play out over time? How will things look a year or five years from now?"

Good decision makers are not blinded by the now. They take the present situation and play it out in their heads to see what happens to it over time.

That nice little summer cottage on the seashore you were thinking of buying—it *is* nice, but how much time will you really spend there, and what about beach erosion, and how many crowds of tourists gather there? Is there something better you can do with that money? Asking simple questions like these is what this law is all about. You've got to challenge the dream of a summer cottage with the reality of what having that summer cottage will really be like when you look ahead without rose-colored glasses.

The easy way to apply this law is just to look ahead. Just *try* to look ahead.

Suppose your marriage is horrible but your kids are wonderful. You're having an affair with someone who gives you everything your spouse doesn't, although you really can't ever spend much time with your lover. Bad decision makers compare the qualities of their spouse with the qualities of their lover, worry about the kids, add it all up, and try to come to a conclusion.

Good decision makers ask, What will happen if I stay married to this person? If I'm staying, won't we try to change things? If so, how much change is possible? How will I feel about my marriage if I get all that change? And what about my lover? Things are great now, but how will the picture look if we marry?

If you look you will see

Sharon and Rick lived near a large electronics manufacturing firm in rural New England. For years, as a convenience to its employees, the company had operated a small grocery/drugstore on-site. One day management decided that this was an unnecessary and unprofitable little sideline and shut it down; what did an electronics firm have to do with running a mom-and-pop store?

Sharon and Rick heard what was happening and saw an opportunity. They invested all their savings and took on debt to open a small supermarket with a drug department across the road from the factory.

At first business was great. But was this a good decision?

Suppose they'd tried to look ahead. They might have thought as follows: "This seems like a good opportunity for us. But what will happen? What about our customers who work at the factory? They're used to extremely low prices and to being able to pick up staples on the way to their cars at the end of the day. Our prices will seem high, and even though management closed down the store, won't there be forces in place to try to bring it back? After all, there's a strong union."

This look ahead—which Sharon and Rick didn't do—turned out to be accurate. The union put pressure on management to bring back the store. Management agreed to do so if it would be a worker-run co-op. Management would have nothing to do with it other than letting the workers have the space for free.

Sharon and Rick lost everything. Not because they weren't able to look ahead, but because they failed to *try* to look ahead. They didn't ask themselves how the situation would play out over time. They confused a great opportunity in the moment for a great opportunity down the road.

Foresight for the rest of us

Let's not kid ourselves. Being able to see ahead, around the corners of time, is another word for brilliance. We can all try. We can all go to the head of the class simply by remembering to try. But doing a great job of looking ahead ain't easy.

So I set myself a challenge. How do ordinary people like you and me look ahead if we lack the total brilliance of the special few?

The answer is that there are certain rules of thumb about how things play out over time. If just asking yourself to look ahead puts you in the top 10 percent, applying these rules of thumb puts you in the top *one* percent.

Are these simplifications? Of course! *Over*simplifications? Not if they're useful.

How to know what's going to happen when you don't know what's going to happen

Look-ahead rule #1: What will happen is what's most likely to happen

This rule says, quite simply, that it's hard to fight the odds and win. If you want to look ahead and guess how your different options will play out, go with the odds. When you're headed for heart surgery, for example, go with the doctor and with the hospital that have more experience and higher success rates. That's obvious.

We get into trouble and start violating Look-ahead rule #1 when we imagine that there are exceptions. We tell ourselves it's different this time. We make up a story for why the odds don't apply now or to us.

But the odds always apply. If you're starting to get involved with someone who has a history of substance abuse, that person has much higher odds of getting in trouble with drugs or alcohol than someone without such a history. If you look ahead, and you're honest with yourself, the odds will tell you what you'll find down the road.

This doesn't mean you can't take risks. It just means that if you do take a risk, you must respect the odds against you. So if you're beautiful, young, and talented, and want to go to Hollywood and become a star like a million other beautiful, young, and talented people, why not? Law #3—*Look for all the good things that can happen*—still applies. But the odds are against you, and if you look ahead you'd have to say that you probably won't become a star. You can still be a wanna-be if you want to be, but you can be a smart wanna-be. Hedge your bets, develop an alternative career, and don't set yourself up for a crash if you don't make it.

In trying to look ahead, just ask yourself what the odds really are, and let that guide your decision.

Look-ahead rule #2: The most striking feature of the option you're considering will always have a huge role in how the decision plays out

Jessica was considering where to go to get her Ph.D. in history. She had two top offers of admission, one from Yale, the other from Cambridge. Yale had a great reputation, but so did Cambridge, and its being in England made Cambridge more attractive to her.

But she forgot to look ahead. *Going* to Cambridge, England, was interesting and romantic, but *studying* there would be something else.

The most striking fact about studying abroad is that you're studying *abroad*—it's *different* there.

It was a disaster. Jessica was an overachiever. She worked hard, but she wasn't a natural genius. Sweat had gotten her far, but the added difficulties of new and often more demanding standards abroad overwhelmed her. The system of super exams there was more than she was ready for. She'd be completely on her own for months with less guidance than she was used to and then suddenly face a test that was harder than she'd ever had in her life. Plus she was competing there with British students who'd grown up in such a system. Jessica eventually had to drop out.

So whenever you're comparing options, look at the most obvious features of each option. Ask what those features will do to you over time. What's a big deal today will probably be a big deal tomorrow. Don't minimize it.

Look-ahead rule #3: Basic structures will stay constant

Every time I hear someone say, "This time it's different," I reach for my gun, metaphorically speaking, because rarely is it different. Yeah, maybe you're one of the brilliant few who have the ability to discern those underground shifts that transform the world before anyone realizes it, but the big, broad, basic realities rarely change, and if you're trying to look ahead, you'd better assume they won't.

What kinds of basic realities am I talking about? Here's one: *It's tough to make a buck.* Even the streets of Silicon Valley are not paved with gold. They're more likely to be paved with the bones of those who thought it was easy to make a buck there. If you're choosing between business opportunities and you smell green somewhere, go for it, but while you're looking ahead never think for a moment it won't be tough to make a buck.

Another is *There's never enough time.* Are you trying to plan ahead? Don't count on finding time.

There's something strikingly solid about people who make good decisions. Because they're aware of how things work, they don't think things will be different this time.

Look-ahead rule #4: Anything that's defective or lacking will grow in importance over time

I call this the pebble-in-the-shoe rule. If you start out with a pebble in your shoe, it won't go away and you won't be able to ignore it. It will stay and the pain will grow. As you try to figure out how your options will play out, look for a problem in any of your options. Then, whatever you do, don't minimize it or assume you'll get used to it.

Suppose you're choosing between two jobs. One's a little better than the other, but it has a very long commute. You say you're tough. You say you're work-oriented. You decide then to ignore the length of the commute as a factor in your decision. If you'd looked ahead properly, you would see that shoe pebbles like a long commute grow more and more and more burdensome.

In trying to see how your options will play out, know that small problems will grow big and big problems will grow horrible.

Look-ahead rule #5: Money is always big

Don't misunderstand me. I'm not saying that money is the be-all and end-all. I'm not saying that money buys happiness. I'm not saying that you should organize your life around money. All I'm doing is coming back to you from discussions with people who have looked back on their good and bad decisions and bringing you the message that good decision makers, when they look ahead, never underestimate the role money plays.

On average, when faced with two job offers, two career choices, two places to live, good decision makers choose the option that gives them more money. They also spend less than bad decision makers, and if they can arrange it they don't spend money at all. For example, they build businesses with other people's money and they forgo vacations; they place their own money in savings.

Say you want to spend your life helping the downtrodden. Good decision makers might very well decide to do this, but they will still observe Look-ahead rule #5: *Money is always big.* They'll still find a way to earn more, spend less, and save more.

All five look-ahead rules are great for those of us who pride ourselves on being realists. They validate our basic approach. I'm not telling you not to be a dreamer or a pioneer, but people who make great decisions don't confuse betting on a long shot with the belief that they're likely to win their bet.

You can sum up all these look-ahead rules with one word, *prudence*. Don't knock it till you've tried it.

Don't confuse my toughness with negativity. If I'm being tough, it's to save hope, not kill it. I'm the biggest optimist in the world. And after all, making great choices is the only way to make your life great.

So maybe being gritty and gimlet-eyed will cause some of your pies to crash down from the sky. But you will save your optimism and hope. Nothing puts hope more at risk than a failure to be realistic about what will really happen if you do whatever it is you're thinking of doing.

In science fiction stories someone always goes back in time, steps on an ant or kills a fly, and that little action sets in motion a chain of events that completely changes the future. We're all time travelers. We stand here at one moment, and the entire future of our personal world rests on our decisions. Look ahead and try to envision the future in which the outcome of your decision will live.

Law #7

Turn Big Decisions into a Series of Little Decisions

What small step can you take toward a decision?

O NE problem with making big decisions is that you have so little to go on. Bad decision makers take a leap into the unknown or do nothing at all. Good decision makers have a secret weapon for balancing out the need to act and the need to know what the hell you're doing. It's a secret weapon we actually use all the time.

I almost had my cat killed last night. But I didn't. And I'm glad.

I made a good decision. But it would've been easy to go the wrong way. You see, my cat's old; she's slow, stiff, and has the occasional bad spell. Most of the time she gets around the house just fine. She climbs all over the furniture. She goes out and sleeps on the lawn. She gets excited about birds outside the window. She has slowed down a little, but if I had to bet I'd say Tippy enjoys her life.

She has hyperthyroidism, and a couple of times her strength and appetite have completely left her. My wife and I vowed that if she fell into one of these states and couldn't be brought out of it, we'd have her put to sleep.

Last night was different. Poor Tippy had a fit, as if she'd suddenly lost all sense of equilibrium. She went from flattening herself on the ground like a cat on the roof of a moving car to flipping herself around like a cat who thinks she's falling and is trying to straighten herself out. It must have been horribly scary for her. I thought, Let me take her to the vet right now and have her put to sleep. No one should go through this torture.

But Law #7—*Turn big decisions into a series of little decisions*—came to our rescue. Putting to sleep a cat you've loved for twenty years is a big decision. Infinitely smaller is the decision to watch her for a while. What if the seizure was a one-time-only occurrence? (Remember Law #3: *Look for all the good things that can happen.*) So I waited and watched. Time passed. Tippy rested a little. And with each minute, she seemed a little better. I decided to see how she did overnight. Another small decision.

At five o'clock in the morning Tippy was fine. To this day, she's still going strong for an old cat. She hasn't had another fit. By breaking that big decision down into small steps, we avoided making a bad and final decision.

How to take one step at a time

This powerful law is of wider use than just dealing with old cats. The most successful generals, statesmen, and business leaders use this law all the time.

Let me make clear what it means to apply this law. It's not about waiting or doing nothing. It's about letting small decisions teach you what the best big decision is.

The name I use for this is the Decisiveness Learning Method (the DLM). The best decision makers understand that you're always involved in a process of continual growth. The decisions of today can always generate new learning. Just ask Steven Jobs, who founded Apple Computer. What happened to him after he left the company? It was what he'd learned from his decisions that made it possible for him to move on to new and more interesting challenges, including returning to Apple to save the company.

Here's the procedure:

Step 1: Lay out your options
As you'll see later, great decision makers always keep their eyes open for overlooked options and always try to create new options.

Really bad decision makers always say, "I only had one choice." So with step 1, see what all of your options are.

Step 2: Ask yourself which of your options can be broken down into smaller steps

This is very important. The obvious answer is to choose the best option. The problem is, you don't know what the best option is. So instead of taking a wild guess, you choose the option that allows you to feel your way along and get information in the process. Don't choose the option that requires you to take one big irrevocable step.

When Tippy had her fit, my first thought was that putting her to sleep was the best option. But I didn't really know what was going on with her. The other option, to wait and watch, had the supreme virtue of allowing me to gain more information.

This amounts to a revolution in decision making. Instead of doing something because you guess it's the best thing to do, you take small steps, get more information, then finally decide. It's not about guess-and-go. It's about learning.

Step 3: Then take that one small, information–generating step

You are making a decision here, but you're making a *small* decision, and it's based not so much on what's best as on what will give you the most information about your situation with the least commitment.

Suppose, for example, you've been offered two big jobs. One job, the one you suspect is your best option, is in London. The other job is here at home, and there's the possibility of checking it out. You can spend a couple of days on-site, unofficially assisting on a project with some of the people you'd be working with. Well then, that's the direction you go in.

Make the small decision to get more information where you can get it. If that second-choice company turns out to be wonderful, you can go with that. If it turns out to be as non-wonderful as you thought it would be, then go with your original assessment.

When information is in short supply, use small decisions to generate the information you need to make your big decision.

Step 4: Take another small step that will give you even more information

If the London job is a big enough decision, take the time to visit it too. Look, I'm realistic. You can't always check out everything, and you can't always break everything into small steps. But people who make great choices *try*. They don't search for that one option that carries its own neon sign saying "This is the great choice to make." They search for small, information-generating steps that will put them way ahead of the curve when it comes to taking the big step.

Step 5: Go ahead and make your big decision when the information you've collected clearly points in one direction or the other. Once you realize you're not going to get more information, delay becomes your enemy.

Many people wait too long. For them there's never enough information. They keep hanging around hoping some piece of the puzzle will drop out of the sky and make everything clear. The people who make great decisions don't spend the most time weighing their options. Instead they take small steps, gain the best information they can, and without delay make their best decision.

Take dating, for example. Dating is one area of our lives where most of us have proved we know this law. Coffee dates before dinner dates. Little dates before big dates. Dates where you make out before dates where you sleep together. Going away for long weekends before you move in together. Take a step, get information, then based on that information take another step. These steps will tell you whether you want to spend a lifetime with this person or whether you want to date someone else.

Prudence in action

It's a remarkable thing about people who make great choices. They *make choices*. They act. They decide. They don't sit around sucking the thumb of uncertainty. They understand that when you have nothing better to go on, action is better than inaction.

But if good decision makers are decisive, they are also prudent. You might think this is a contradiction. Prudence says wait and watch. Decisiveness says go. How do you reconcile the two?

This law brings them into a working partnership. You prudently get a bit of information. You decisively take a small step. You prudently get more information. You decisively take another step. You never make more than the minimum necessary commitment that will help you see farther over the horizon.

Taking it out for a spin

The idea that you *act* as a way to make better decisions is very powerful. That's probably why it's so popular among people who make great decisions. The Decisiveness Learning Method exemplifies this principle. Another version of this principle is called the *trial run*.

Here's what you do. Maybe you're stuck in a lousy job and you don't know whether to look for a new one or go back to school. Maybe you own a business and you could expand it or leave things as they are for now.

Take your options for a trial run. For one whole week, beginning Monday morning, live as if you have firmly decided on one of your options. For example, live as if you've absolutely decided to marry the safer, sweeter, but slightly more geeky of the two people you've been seeing. Or live as if you've decided to go back to school. Live as if you won't expand your business.

Psychologically what you're doing is locking yourself in a room with one option for one week.

What happens during this trial run? Does your anxiety subside? Do you start feeling happier? Or do you have an increasingly gnawing, queasy feeling? Is this week a good week for you or a bad week?

On Sunday night do an assessment. Where would you rate that option, on a scale from ten at the highest end of the positive scale to minus ten at the lowest end of the negative scale?

The next Monday morning, begin a trial run for your other alternative. Live for one week as if *that's* what you're going to do. See how you feel over the course of the week, and on Sunday night, again do an assessment. You've just road-tested your decision. Go with the option that feels better.

Sometimes things aren't as blindingly clear as you'd hoped. Check out the feelings your trial run stirred up in you. Let's say you were trying to choose between two jobs. One job was better in every way except for the money, but the money turned out to be a huge issue as you lived with your options. Maybe you have to live with less money now to make more money later. Maybe the job with more money is in a high-tax state. Maybe you need to give yourself a chance to say that the money isn't as important as you'd first thought. Your trial run brought up an issue you needed to probe into more deeply.

Maybe after two weeks of road testing you can't find any difference between your two alternatives. What do you do?

If you don't have to choose right now, give yourself more time. Law #2: *Don't decide until you're ready!*

If there's a deadline for deciding and you feel equally good about both, why not flip a coin? That's a perfectly responsible decision-making device when you feel equally good about both alternatives. So flip that coin and go, man, go.

When you've gathered all of the information you can and you're still in doubt, action is better than inaction. That puts you on the road to being a great decision maker.

Everyone knows that you should try to get more information to make better decisions. The secret weapon of great decision makers is that sometimes you should try to make more small decisions to get better information.

Law #8

You Always Have Better Options

What are better options beyond those you've checked out?

I LOVE Dr. Spock. My parents relied on him for advice when I was born, and my wife and I relied on him for advice with our own kids. He was our baby doctor in a book.

But he had a little tip—valuable as it was in context—that unintentionally exemplifies how good people become bad decision makers. Let's say you're taking your child shopping for a new coat. If he's six, he's too young to pick out his own coat, but he's going to want to have some say in the decision. What do you do? Shut him out of the process and make him feel powerless? Give all the coat-buying power to a six-year-old?

No. Spock wisely suggests that you select two coats you think are acceptable and say to your kid, "Which of these two coats do you want?" as if those were the only two coats in the world to choose from.

I've seen this work a million times. I used the same tactic to get my kids to go to bed. I didn't say, "It's time to go to bed," because they always had their own opinion on the matter. Instead I'd say, "Do you want me to carry you to bed in my arms or on my shoulders?" If they should have an opinion about whether or not to go to bed in the first place, I'd ignore them and talk about the attractive features of the two different ways of being carried off to bed. They got distracted by the options I offered them and fell for it every time.

That's great for parenting. It's terrible when you're an adult and life hands you a limited menu of options and you respond as if those options are all there is.

There are always more options

This is one of those times when a basic weakness of ours confronts a natural strength. The basic weakness is the ease with which we get hypnotized by our existing options. Thank God we have the natural strength of looking for new options that more than compensates for this, if we let it. It's not really anything special. Thinking of new possibilities is just another word for basic intelligence. We just have to let ourselves be smart.

A guy walks up to you on the street late at night. "Your money or your life," he says, smart psychologist that he is. What do you do? If you're like most of us, you're suddenly and terrifyingly frozen into a narrow and rigid universe where there are two and only two options. Of the two, which will we choose?

The great Mira Kirshenbaum, my life partner and the person I turn to whenever I need help with a decision, faced a very similar situation. With the instinct of a great decision maker, she showed the value of this law: *you always have better options.*

She was sixteen and lived in a tall modern apartment house on the Lower East Side of Manhattan. Mira came home late one evening. A young man got in the elevator with her, pulled a knife, and said, "Come with me into the stairwell or I'll kill you right here." Mira guessed what was in store for her in that stairwell.

Again, like all of us when faced with a decision, she was offered an extremely rigid, narrow range of options. Rape or death.

Mira, a street kid, said, "Listen, my mother's not home. Why should we go to the stairwell? We can go to my apartment." She acted cool, friendly. She pulled a switcheroo on him. She offered *him* a rigid, narrow range of options. Sex with risk of being discovered in the stairwell, or sex without that risk in an apartment. He got hypnotized by limited options and opted for the apartment, of course.

What Mira knew was that her mother, a woman from the old

country, was standing at the apartment door the whole time waiting for her as she always did and that she would open the door the minute she heard the elevator arrive at her floor. When the elevator door opened and Mira stepped out, her mother immediately started yelling at her for being late. The guy heard the yelling, got scared, and pressed the down button.

Mira did something very risky, and I would never recommend anyone following literally what she did.

The point I'm trying to make is that you can save yourself from making bad decisions by always, always giving yourself more options. The more convinced you are that there aren't any other options, the more determined you should be to discover more options.

You just have to look

If you can't think of more options, take the time to search for more. Ask for help. I'll show you how to generate new options in a moment. But know this: If you go with the options that first present themselves to you, you are in serious danger of heading toward a bad decision. You've given up control to a tiny menu of possibilities. Why do that? If you had only one night in Paris, wouldn't you consider eating at a restaurant better than the one closest to your hotel?

Good decision makers always say things like:

- *"I'm sure we can come up with another option."*

- *"Are these our only options?"*

- *"Let's not decide until we come up with more options."*

I passionately believe in focusing on the power of great decisions to create great lives. Decision making is all about making life wonderful. There *are* pies in the sky, but let them not blind us to the horrible consequences of bad decision making. And I promise you: analyze almost every bad decision—every really stupid, bone-headed decision—and you'll find someone who never looked beyond a limited set of options.

Bad options result in bad decisions

Talk to people who've committed a violent crime. It's usually the same story. They get it into their head to commit an act of murder, for example, *and that's it*. It's not the same as being impulsive. These people often have plenty of time, more than enough to fulfill the legal requirement of "forethought." The reason they do such stupid things is that once they get an idea in their heads, they neither challenge it nor offer themselves an alternative.

As one young murderer chillingly said, "I just *X*'ed out any other alternative," meaning that he refused even to consider anything else.

Here we are, in our nice suburban lives, thinking it's a big deal to get a speeding ticket, and it's easy for us to feel superior to these young criminals. But don't be too arrogant.

Look back on some bad decision you made. Pick one at random. Tune in to that moment in your personal history. Tune in to what was going on in your head. Listen. I'll bet you'll hear yourself saying things like "I just don't have an alternative" or "I just have to do this." Maybe you'll hear nothing, just the inner silence that fills us when we get some idea in our heads about doing something and that's it. The boat you just had to have. The motorcycle. The trip to Paris when you were unemployed. The tennis bracelet from Tiffany. The time you and some inappropriate person said, "Let's get married," and you went ahead and did it.

They always seem like such good ideas. You just *X* out the alternatives.

Here's what you need to do. Set your radar to watch out for any of the following dangerous situations:

• an idea pops into your head as *the* thing to do

• it seems as though there are only one or two alternatives

  • someone forces your hand by making it seem as though you
    have only one or two options.

Now be careful here. At this moment you might be feeling
very proud of yourself. You're realistic. You know what's what.

You also may be in the worst danger of your life. When
you believe your options are limited, that's precisely when you
must generate new options. They exist. You will be able to find
them.

You're condo hunting and you find one that might be okay,
and the real estate agent says that you have to make an offer today
because someone else is interested. Sounds like limited options,
doesn't it? Then that means there *are* further options and you need
to find them.

What further options? Well, this isn't the last condo on earth. If
it's not exactly what you want and if you haven't really checked out
both this condo and what else you might get, how do you know
it's worth pursuing at all?

As for your losing it, how do you know you'll lose it if you
don't make an offer that day? First of all, there may not actually be
other people. If you wait and other interested buyers show up, so
what? You make a bid. As long as you don't bid more than you're
willing to pay, what's the problem?

Molly's story

Speaking of real estate, a young woman right out of college was
working as a real estate agent. Both of her parents had been in real
estate, and she wanted to make it. But she wasn't doing very well.
Finally, one day her boss came to her and said, "Molly, I have to let
you go."

Now I love this part. Molly said, "No you don't." It blew his
mind. He couldn't even understand what she was saying at first and
thought she'd misunderstood him. "No," Molly said, "I know you
think you have to let me go but you don't."

"Molly, I'm firing you."

"No you're not."

The boss couldn't even have imagined anyone responding this

way. Tears, yes. Pleading, yes. But not the simple refusal to accept what he considered a nonnegotiable situation.

Molly thought fast and presented some kind of deal where she'd stay and work without a draw. She felt very strongly that she was on the verge of making a couple of sales. Her boss was smart enough to realize that you don't fire a salesperson who not only won't take no for an answer but won't even see the no.

You can learn a lesson from Molly that will help you keep this law in your memory. *You don't have to know what your other options are to know that you have other options.* Don't make the mistake of starting out saying, "I don't have a choice unless somehow I find a choice." It's the other way around. "I always have a choice unless after ample searching I've exhausted all the choices."

And never think you've exhausted all the choices.

If you're facing a big decision and you feel your options are few, slow the process down. If someone's holding you to a deadline, refuse to accept the deadline. If you're going to lose an option because of an artificial deadline, then lose it, because you never want to be put in the position of being forced to choose among limited options. Then, if nothing else, find someone with experience and wisdom in the area of your particular decision. I guarantee he or she will present better options to you than you ever imagined.

Law #9

Get What You Need to Feel Safe

What are you doing to take care of your safety needs?

WHEN it comes to making big decisions, most of us spend too much time worrying about how things can go wrong and not enough time actually creating safety for ourselves.

Safety is not a state. It's a trade-off. You can have a lot of safety if you move extremely slowly, take little risk, turn away from whatever's new and unfamiliar, and put most of your energy into trying to gain as much control as possible. Or you can move, make things happen, shake things up, risk rejection, charge across frontiers, and in the process possibly lose a great deal of safety.

Most people fall into one of these two camps. Either they're victims of the Saint Sebastian syndrome, or they have a case of the Icarus complex. Which camp do you fall into? It's not a question of one being better than the other. It's a question of knowing how you work, so you can create real safety for yourself when it comes to making decisions.

The Saint Sebastian syndrome
Saint Sebastian is the guy you recognize in paintings because he is wearing a halo, his body shot full of arrows. That was how he was martyred.

You have the Saint Sebastian syndrome if you approach decisions afraid of being shot by some unknown arrow of trouble. Danger lurks on every side, and your fear makes sense to you, because you're constantly aware of all the different ways things can go wrong. In fact your understanding of how things can go wrong makes you feel smart and powerful.

Knowing where danger lurks is good. Fearing that danger lurks everywhere is bad. When it comes to making decisions, people with the Saint Sebastian syndrome get in trouble when they get to the point where they can't move forward.

The Icarus complex

People suffering from the Icarus complex are in the opposite position. Icarus was the son of Daedalus, the master craftsman of Greek mythology, who made for himself and his son pairs of wings out of wax and feathers. Overconfident, Icarus flew higher and higher in the sky. As he flew closer to the sun, the wax melted, his wings fell apart, and Icarus tumbled to his death.

Those of us with the Icarus complex act first and worry later. If the hot sun should happen to melt the wax of our hasty decisions, we contemplate our "should'ves" as we fall to earth.

People with the Icarus complex don't take their safety needs seriously enough. "If I worry about stuff, I just won't do anything," they say. Or, "What could possibly go wrong?" Or, "Don't worry—whatever happens I can deal with it."

Discovering, and meeting, your safety needs

The Icarus complex and the Saint Sebastian syndrome are two ways of getting into trouble. With one you don't pay enough attention to safety. With the other you pay too much attention.

It's time we stopped feeling trapped by one approach or the other. Whichever approach you're stuck in, it's time you got what you needed so you could move forward like an Icarus, without fear of being attacked from every side the way Saint Sebastian was, but without Icarus's foolhardiness. Once again we meet our three themes of prudence, action, and the hope for wonderfulness.

People who make good decisions have a surprising and straightforward solution to this seemingly insurmountable problem. They say essentially, "Yes, dangers may be unlimited, but for all practical purposes if I identify the *one thing* I need to feel safe moving forward and make sure I get *that,* I'll feel free to go ahead with my decision."

Now understand this: They don't look for every safety need. They look for the one thing they need to feel safe enough to move forward.

So that's what you and I will do right now. I'll help you discover your one safety need as you face some big, scary decision.

Here are the most common things people actually need to get real safety for themselves in different situations. As I describe each one, ask yourself, "If I got that for myself, would I feel safe enough to make my decision the way I'd like?"

If you feel you have most of these different safety needs, you're probably a Saint Sebastian. You see danger as coming from too many places. The solution for you is to force yourself to say which one need will make you feel safest if you met it.

If you feel you have none of these safety needs, you're probably an Icarus. You're at risk of putting yourself in danger without realizing it. In that case, force yourself to say which safety need feels like it's probably the biggest.

Safety need #1: "I need to know the worst thing that can happen, and I need to know that it's extremely unlikely, or that I have control over whether it happens, or that even if it does happen I'll be okay."

Talk about statements you hear from the lips of people who make good decisions. "What's the worst that can happen if I do this?" they say repeatedly. For many people, zeroing in on the worst that can happen is their number one safety issue and gives them everything they need to take care of themselves.

The brave men and women who served as operatives behind the lines for the U.S. secret forces during World War II used this approach. This is the reason for the cyanide capsule. The worst thing that could happen to them wasn't being killed. This was war. Men and women risked their lives every day. Far worse than being killed was being captured, tortured, and forced to give up the names of fellow operatives. The cyanide capsule was every spy's assurance that the worst that could happen wouldn't happen.

But let's not be overdramatic. No matter what kind of decision you make, asking what's the worst that can happen can make it safe enough for you to go forward. Going out on a blind date. What's the worst that can happen? The other person's horrible. So you claim you have a headache and leave early. Starting a small business. What's the worst that can happen? Maybe it's that you could lose all your money. So you take out loans and incorporate. That way not all the money you lose is yours, and you're not liable for every bit of debt.

Asking what's the worst that can happen is wonderful medicine for people suffering from either the Saint Sebastian syndrome or the Icarus complex.

If you're afraid of trouble coming at you from all directions as happened to poor Saint Sebastian, asking what's the worst that can happen will focus you on the most important danger. You'll feel that much more comfortable letting go of worry about less important dangers.

And if you have the Icarus complex, here's how to temper your daring.

- Think about your different options. For each option, *ask what's the worst that can happen realistically*. If it's really not very likely, it's probably not worth factoring into your decision.

- *Ask yourself if you can protect yourself against having the worst thing happen*. This is why mountain climbers have ropes. It's why newlyweds have prenuptial agreements. In fact there are very few efforts human beings embark on for which they can't buy protection against the worst thing that could happen.

- *Ask yourself if you'll overcome the worst thing*. If you let yourself fall in love with someone and they break your heart, are you really destroyed forever? Lots of times if we think clearly about the "worst thing," we realize that our panic is out of proportion to the real but survivable difficulties we'd face.

Will being able to focus on the worst thing that can happen give you what you need to feel safe? Focusing on the worst thing that can happen is a way to make your safety needs manageable. If the "worst thing" turns out to be not so bad, the dangers facing you shrink in importance. As long as there's only one worst thing, you can focus on getting protection, instead of having to look everywhere for safety.

Safety need #2: "I need to feel I can back out at the last minute if necessary."

Think of this as Icarus with a parachute. With this safety need, as long as you know where the exits are and know you can get to an exit, you've gotten what you need to feel safe enough to move forward.

Don, like Icarus, was the son of a famous father, a well-known real-estate developer. His father had made and lost fortunes during the booms and busts of Boston commercial real estate. Don was brought up to enter the family business but he hated it. He felt almost paralyzed as he approached every transaction. Afraid that people would think him stupid, he came up with elaborate explanations for why caution was smart. But like McClellan, the general Lincoln fired for never fighting, Don just never made deals.

Soon Don started feeling very bad about himself. Through the help of a therapist, he came to understand that he needed to feel he could bail out fast if necessary. That was his safety issue. Clearly real estate was a bad match for someone like him. Every real estate project is a juggernaut, and guys like Don are allergic to juggernauts.

It was clear that Don would never get his biggest safety need met by staying in real estate; there was just no bailout potential there. Then he got the idea of managing his family's considerable stock-market portfolio. Here Don came into his own. Making risky decisions in the stock market was no problem for Don. Because of the extreme liquidity of transactions he could easily bail out of a situation if the sun started melting his wing wax.

Will knowing how to get out of your decision give you what you need to feel safe? If this describes you, then you'll get your safety need met if you look for situations for which an exit can be found in advance.

Safety need # 3: "I need to feel everyone I care about approves of my decision."

Vera, like Don, was a portfolio manager for a famous Boston-based family of mutual funds. Unlike Don, Vera had grown up poor. She managed a portfolio well into the nine figures, yet when it came to her personal life she couldn't shake the sense that twenty bucks was still a lot of money. How did Vera get to the point emotionally where she felt able to pull the trigger on multimillion-dollar decisions?

She started out as an analyst. That was easy for Vera, just a lot of researching and number crunching. She did so well that she was offered her first portfolio to manage. When she panicked and said no without thinking, her wise boss quickly said: "You won't be alone, you know. We don't work like that. You'll have your own team, and we kind of encourage—well, force actually—people in your position to consult with other fund managers. If anything you'll be complaining about how we're interfering with you."

Those words turned the key in the lock for Vera. So what if she'd be the fund manager? She wouldn't be alone. She wouldn't have to make any decisions that a bunch of other people hadn't approved of first. The possibility of losses, of poor performance, didn't faze her. As long as others were with her she felt safe.

Will it make you feel safe to know that people who matter to you approve of your decision? If this describes you, then you'll get your safety need met if you have your kitchen cabinet of advisers and consultants to take along with you as you go through the process of making your decisions. Just get these people on board with you, and go.

Safety need #4: "I need to understand what game I'm in and how to win it."

Many people who make good decisions get safety for themselves by pretending life is a game and figuring out the rules for playing and winning. Melanie had dreamed of starting her own little magazine. Not a 'zine but a real money-making magazine, however small. She wanted to do this because she loved the music business, and starting a magazine could give her a place in that business.

For any of her decisions, though, Melanie needed to know how to win that game. Take dating, for example. She used to think that the game there was to get a guy, any guy, to like her. But that kept playing out badly. She kept getting involved with guys she didn't like and who didn't like her once they found out she wasn't being herself. Then she understood that in order to win the game she needed to find out as much as possible about the guy in advance and show him who she really was. She felt safe when she understood the real game.

When it came to her magazine—one devoted to covering the alternative rock scene—she discovered that the game was pulling together a target audience for advertisers.

It's not that Melanie wanted to be a businesswoman, but understanding her particular game as a business made her feel safe enough to go forward and make it all happen. Instead of spending her time at the beginning developing content, Melanie talked to prospective advertisers, asking them about the kinds of people they'd like to reach.

Will knowing exactly what game you're really in give you what you need to feel safe? If you can relate to this, then you'll get the safety you need to move forward if you understand how things really work—and most of all how success really works—in whatever option you're thinking of choosing.

Safety is a huge and scary topic when it comes to making decisions. We don't want to be paralyzed, but we don't want to be foolhardy. It's easy to be overwhelmed. People who make good decisions walk the line between fear and foolhardiness. If you think about every possible danger, you'll be paralyzed. If you ignore possible dangers, you'll crash and burn. But if you remember to ask yourself what's the one thing you need to feel safe and make sure you give yourself that, you'll have taken the best single step to care for your safety needs.

Law #10

Do What You Really Want

Are you sure you've let your heart's desire hold sway?

L ET's get one thing straight right away. I don't want any misunderstanding about this. Great decision makers don't just run around doing whatever they want. You won't make great decisions if you always do whatever you damned please.

Are we clear on that? Good. We've given responsibility its due.

When you sort through good choices and bad choices, you keep finding over and over that people who make good choices ask themselves what they really want and give a lot of weight to what they really want.

In an alarming number of bad decisions, I find that the person never asked himself what he really wanted. Great decisions are built on the foundation of your own true desires, of what you want for yourself.

Lots of people, unfortunately, get so swept up by events, by the momentum of their lives, by the clamor of other people, by sheer habit, by fear of failure, by fear of embarrassment, that this crucial issue gets lost. *What do you want in yourself? for yourself?*

People who make great choices are just like the rest of us. They too don't always know the answers to these questions at the beginning. They too have their responsibilities. *But* they don't make big decisions until they dig down and reach the place where they see what they want.

Digging down to your heart's desire

Here's where it gets hairy: what you *say* you want, what you *assume* you want, isn't the same as what you really, really want. That's where people get into trouble.

I'm lucky enough to have witnessed two women in a support group for people facing life-changing decisions. Each was pregnant, and the big decision each faced was whether she should go back to work after the baby was born.

One, Carol, was a management consultant. The other, Lizzie, was in advertising. Both had husbands who earned a decent living. Both were in their late thirties, expecting their first babies. When they started talking, Carol had decided that when her baby came she'd stay home for at least the next several years to raise it. Lizzie had decided that she'd go back to work as soon as possible.

They both said the same thing, in almost the same words. "I've thought about it and it's really best for everyone. Besides, it's what I want."

Carol went on to say, "Look, I just think a child needs its mother. No stranger can give the kid what a mother can. I don't want to have kids for someone else to raise. Of course I don't have family nearby to help out either, but even if I did I'd still want to experience being there for all the special moments. Otherwise why have kids?"

Lizzie said, "I know how you feel. I felt the same way myself. But we need the money, and I don't know if I'll ever be able to pick up my career where I left it if I walk away now. I know there will be things I miss. But I'm sorry, I really do believe in quality time. My kid will know who his mother is and I'll feel I've got a life."

They kept talking, though not to change each other's mind. That wasn't the point of the group. They just wanted to help each other troubleshoot potential pitfalls on the paths they were about to take.

As they talked, that week and the next, new information came out. Carol initially had said her husband "supported" her decision to stay home with the baby, but it turned out that he was actually pressuring her very strongly to stay at home. While it was true that Carol really wanted to be a good mother, she spoke of a troubled relationship with her own mother, who was demanding and cold to Carol even though she had been a stay-at-home mom. Carol very much wanted to give her child what she didn't get from her mother: love and acceptance and attention.

Lizzie had talked about her career, but the truth was that she'd wrestled with low self-esteem for quite a while. Saying "I work in advertising" always gave her a boost, but in fact she found her work as a traffic manager draining, meaningless, and frequently humiliating. Her mother had died when Lizzie was seven. Lizzie felt she'd missed out on being mothered. That left a hole in her heart. Not feeling good about herself, she was afraid she wouldn't know what to do if she was called upon to be a mother herself. Motherhood scared her.

Over the next few weeks Carol and Lizzie kept talking outside of the group over cups of herbal tea. Their conversation soon took on a strange dynamic, as I found out from their detailed reports. Each told me about how incredibly supportive the other was. Oversupportive. So incredibly supportive that both women became uneasy. Carol told me, "If Lizzie is so in love with my staying home with my baby, why doesn't she do it herself?" Lizzie told me, "It's not just that Carol says it's okay, but she makes me feel as if it's infinitely better, my going back to work instead of leaving the job to become a stay-at-home mom. I get the feeling almost that she's living vicariously through me."

I started getting the sense that both these women were somehow in denial about what they really wanted—maybe they'd never bothered to ask themselves what was their hearts' desire. If they didn't get in touch with their real desires fast, they could both make decisions they'd regret.

You see, having a bunch of opinions and attitudes and confidently saying what you want is not the same as actually, honestly, and deeply checking in with yourself to see what you really want.

Carol and Lizzie each stimulated the other to a crisis. "I should be so happy," each said to me, "but I'm not. How can that be?"

"Look," I said to each one, "you've dug yourself into a certain position, but I don't think you've asked yourself what you really want. I understand—you know what you think you should want. You know what other people want for you. You know what you're afraid of. You know what's easiest. But have you dug down deep within to see what it is you want when you're absolutely honest with yourself?"

Here's what each came up with. Carol, who'd tentatively decided to be a stay-at-home mom, realized that she was afraid of having a fight with her husband, she wanted to one-up her mother, and she was afraid that going back to work would make her just like her mother. She'd told herself she was tired, but not so tired that she needed a ten- or twenty-year break from her career. She'd started telling friends she was going to stay home, so Carol felt embarrassed about publicly changing her plans.

The fact was that Carol really wanted to go back to work after a few months. She liked being a consultant. She liked making her own money. While she was thrilled at the thought of being a mother, she very much dreaded the thought of being trapped at home and not having her own life.

Lizzie was the opposite. Motherhood frightened her. She was afraid she wouldn't be up to the challenge. But the thought of committing to it full-time also thrilled her.

It's scary to think that you're on the verge of making a decision and you're tending toward one option when in fact what you really want is the other. Carol and Lizzie make clear how we fall into the trap of blinding ourselves to what we really want.

A decision is not just about how things "work out." It's about getting what you really want. When your desires are satisfied, not when events work out smoothly or successfully, then a decision is proved successful.

Connecting to what you really want

Here are three lessons to help you connect to what you really want when you're facing any big decision:

➔ **You don't just make a decision. You live a decision.**
It's like buying a bed. The concept may be great, but if it doesn't feel good when you lie in it then it's no good for you. When you try to connect with what you really want, focus on the experience, not the concept. Focus on how it will genuinely feel to carry out the decision, not on what you think it's supposed to be.

You can't get too concrete. When you think about living your decision, how will you feel Sunday night, Monday morning, all throughout Wednesday and Friday afternoon? The decision you really want is the decision you can live with day in and day out.

➔ **You've got to ask yourself what you would want if none of the people in your life were in the picture.**
Let's face it, we really do want the people in our lives to be happy. We're happy when they're happy, but that's not the bedrock of what we really want most.

For example, your spouse or lover wants to have children and live in the country. You don't want children and want to live in the city. For you, a life with children is like a rowboat piled with anvils. You vastly prefer the peace and quiet of a childless life in the big city. Asking yourself "What would I want if I were completely on my own?" is a very effective way to get in touch with your true desires.

➔ **Get outside of the momentum of the world to see what you really want.**
We often lose touch with what we want because early on we set events in motion and then we're carried away by them. At work, for example, there might be a project you think you'd like to take on. Heading it up might be good for your career, so you start talking to people. They like it. They climb on board. They give you good ideas. They start getting invested in it. Just one problem: the more you learn about it, the less you want to do it. It's just that there are all those damn people who've gotten up a head of steam. Meetings that have been set up, contracts that have been negotiated, dreams that have been launched are no substitute for your true desires.

People who make great decisions may not know themselves better than anyone else. You don't need to be the king or queen of self-knowledge. Simply refuse to let any thought, any belief, any person contaminate your clear-eyed sense of what you want.

Think of it this way: Imagine a room full of people talking their heads off. In the middle of that room is you, and with the still small voice of your true self you are saying, clearly and simply, what you really want. But all those other voices!

Those voices are real. But they're not your voice.

People who make bad choices get distracted, confused, deflected by other voices. People who make good choices never let anyone else's voice drown out their own attempts to discover what they really want.

Law #11

If It Ain't Simple, It Ain't Gonna Work

Are you making things more complicated than they need to be?

As a trial lawyer, Donna struck terror in the hearts of companies whose unsafe products injured consumers. Donna was a warrior, and a successful one. But when it came to her wedding, she had the same orange-blossom fantasies many women have. She wanted the big, beautiful, knock-'em-dead wedding of her dreams. A million guests. Swans, helicopters, strolling musicians, boats—Busby Berkeley meets Cecil B. DeMille.

She didn't want just a big wedding, she wanted a complicated one. Wedding consultants offered her packages, but she wanted a custom-tailored wedding. It was as if she wore a sign saying, "Let's make everything as complicated as possible."

How would you guess things turned out? Well, let me ask you this: What happened the last time you tried to coordinate a Friday evening out with three other couples? Did everything go as smoothly as first conceived?

Maybe it would've been fine if Donna had been a take-things-as-they-come person. But type-A litigators aren't usually like this. So as the countless predictable little disasters unfolded, Donna flipped out. The disasters had two main causes. First, believe it or not, the wedding and reception took place at three different venues. Then, the timetable for music and food and entertainment was complex and down-to-the-minute. The logistics were just impossible, and there was no way to rehearse them. Guests, musicians, and caterers all kept showing up at the wrong place at the wrong time.

This was an unnecessary disaster based on a bad decision. The reason good decision makers always keep things simple is that they understand the power and endless applicability of Murphy's Law— whatever can go wrong will go wrong, and the more ways things can go wrong, the more likely things are to go wrong.

How to lure yourself away from doom

It should be so simple, always basing your decisions on what's simple. The reason we need help remembering this law—*If it ain't simple, it ain't gonna work*—is that we're so easily seduced into making things complicated. Here are some beliefs that lure us into complications:

- We believe that an elaborate justification for what we're about to do seems smarter than a simple justification.

- We think we can take a complicated situation and make it work.

- We believe that only a very complicated picture does justice to our complicated sense of reality, and so simplicity would be a betrayal of our reality.

- We believe that some highly complicated option, like Donna's wedding, is just so damned attractive that we downplay the complications.

- It's flattering to think we can juggle complications with ease. We don't want to think of ourselves as unable to handle anything except the simple.

But if you listen to people who make good decisions, you hear them say things like this all the time:

- "Well, which option is simpler? Let's just go with that."

- "I don't want to do that. It'll make things too complicated."

- "There's got to be a simpler way to do this."

- "If you want to convince me, you've got to make your case a lot simpler."

Following this law is easy, but you have to be determined. Every decision maker is like a conventioneer in a roomful of seductresses, and complications are the seductresses. If you resist temptation, you'll be okay, but this requires you to do something that isn't obvious. Surrounded by seductive complications, you've got to hold fast to the idea that simplicity itself is wonderful. And that's hard, because simplicity isn't sexy. It doesn't make you look good to walk into a room with simplicity on your arm.

In the world of decision making, winners opt for simplicity every time. They hang tough and make it a priority in and of itself.

Think about the last bad decision you made. There's a good chance that somewhere, somehow, you got mired in complications. People who've made bad decisions are always saying, "I should've made things simpler."

Let me break this down for you, so this law is perfectly clear.

→ *One priority is better than many priorities.*
You're thinking of going on vacation, and this is the big one—the first time in years you've had a full four weeks to yourself. There's so much you could do, and so much you'd like to do. But those who have the best vacations focus on one priority.

Imagine what a great vacation you could have if *rest* were your one priority.

Or your one priority could be to visit Machu Picchu. Great! A good use of a once-in-a-lifetime vacation, if this is your cup of tea.

We feel so deprived and there's so much we'd like to do. The temptation to festoon a four-week holiday with a wild assortment of different activities can be overwhelming. It's like packing—you always think you can fit in one more thing.

Watch out! The people who have the best vacations will be the people who wanted the fewest, simplest things from their vacation.

This principle applies everywhere. I talk to young people thinking of starting careers, and I've noticed that people who have one priority—money, or living in the country, or helping others— end up happy with their career choice. People who have a lot of priorities, perhaps because they have successful parents or siblings to compare themselves to, tend to dither, flounder, and suffer. They can't make good decisions until they pare down their priorities.

Few principles are as important in business as this one. Steve Case at AOL has done such a great job because he has one priority: create a point on the internet through which everything else must flow. No distractions. No confusions. It's not easy, but nothing creates the likelihood that something wonderful will happen more powerfully than having one priority.

➜ *A simple procedure for deciding is better than a complicated one.* I worked on *Too Good to Leave, Too Bad to Stay,* a book about making the decision to stay or leave a troubled relationship. In the process I discovered something amazing. People who made bad decisions, or got stuck unable to decide at all (which is a bad decision in itself), used very complicated procedures for figuring out what to do. Typically they generated long lists of pros and cons.

What to put on the lists and what weight to give the items on the list always got complicated. People would have long conversations with friends, because talking to others is a procedure for making decisions, and all their different friends often had different opinions, and then things got even more complicated.

But look at what people did who made that difficult decision successfully. They asked one question at a time. For example, "Do we like each other?" No? Then *that's it*. If we don't like each other, how can we love each other? *Like* is the foundation of *love*.

The point isn't that this is such a brilliant question. It is a simple, honest, sturdy question. It cuts to the heart of an important truth. What more simple procedure can there be than asking one simple question at a time?

Some say it's too simple, but everyone who complains about simplicity is really indulging in self-flattery: "I'm too smart and deep and wonderful to be satisfied with simplicity. Someone with a giant heart and mind like mine can handle complications." The same people who complain about oversimplification tend to be those who get stuck unable to decide and then make the wrong choice over and over.

What are some simple recipes for making the best decision? It depends on the situation.

- If it's a decision that involves technical issues, ask three experts and go with the majority. Or go with the expert with the most experience with your particular problem.

- If it's a decision that involves more uncertainty than usual, go with whatever looks best (what procedure could be simpler than that?), but take things one small step at a time. Remember the Decisiveness Learning Method (page 88), and let it rule.

- If all else fails, or before you try anything else, use Law #1: *Focus on the most important thing.* Whatever is the top issue in your decision, exclude everything else and let that rule.

- If you've agonized over a decision for a long time and can't choose between two options, ask the friend whose opinion you respect the most to decide for you. Even if you disagree, at least it gets you thinking and moving.

→ *An option that's simple to implement is better than one that's complicated to implement.*
This is where Donna got into trouble. With most of our decisions, we're not finished when we make the decision. The next thing we have to do is make the decision *work*.

Let's say you're trying to choose between two new jobs. One's good, the other's dazzling. Well, before you get excited, ask yourself what's the job within the job at your dazzling option. What has to happen, in other words, for you to do well at the dazzling job? How complicated will that be? How many things will have to go right, and how much control will you have over those things? For example, what if there's a lot of politics at your dazzling job and people there who don't want you to succeed? The good job isn't the one that's easy for you to say yes to, it's the one that's easy for you to succeed at.

The key to remembering this law and applying it successfully is resisting the seduction of the complicated. Experiments have been done in which a person is given an explanation of a scientific principle. Those who don't know the principle are given two different explanations, a simple one that's correct and a complicated one that's false. Over and over again people vote for the false explanation. Because it was complicated, they fell for it. Complication feels right to us, and that's wrong.

Do you want to be a winner in business? Always go into every meeting with a very simple option you're promoting and a very complicated explanation for why it's good. You'll win both ways. Just never forget that real winners always give simplicity their ultimate loyalty.

Never overlook the option that's simpler to understand and carry out than the others. If you find one option that is simple to understand and carry out, embrace it. You'll be surprised at how often success and satisfaction are brought about this way.

Law #12

Have a Hopeful Heart and a Cautious Head

Have you balanced hoping for the best with protecting yourself from the worst?

WHO'S right—optimists? pessimists? Or is there some perfect attitude in between that's the perfect one to have when you make a decision?

Or does it even matter?

Once again, Dr. Foster is happy to bring you good news. There *is* a right attitude to have, an attitude all of us have the potential to develop within ourselves.

The right attitude brings optimism and pessimism into a natural harmony and balance, each coming into its own like two four-year-olds playing nicely together in a sandbox, each thriving because the other is present.

In a dialogue between your heart and your head, do you know who's right? They both are.

Out of balance

Most of us haven't found a balance between optimism and pessimism. We're like either Emma or Josh. Watch how each is in danger because each emphasizes only one attitude. Which one are you like?

The optimist

Emma is an optimist. She particularly struggles with this at her job, where she's hiring manager for a large inner-city-based high-tech manufacturing firm. Her company has a constant need for new assembly workers. Training costs are high, employee failure costs are high, but the company's demands for new employees are relentless.

Almost all entry-level applicants have problems or deficits in their backgrounds. Emma wants to believe the best about people. She wants to feel that every new hire could one day become CEO. She wants to trust their stories of how they ran into difficulties and why these difficulties are behind them. She wants to change the world through the transformative magic of her hiring power.

Emma is an idealist working in a high-tech world built on a substrate of idealism, and in principle there's nothing wrong with that. We need idealists. In practice, though, Emma too often finds herself hiring questionable applicants, usually with the annotation "Should be okay, but keep an eye on him." Too many of them are not okay. As her boss realizes all too well, more new hires crash and burn than should be the case.

So Emma's always at war with herself. She keeps saying to herself, "I've got to get tough. I can't let them walk all over me." She fantasizes about being the narrow-eyed, cynical-lipped pessimist that's her alter ego; it would never hire anyone who wasn't almost guaranteed to work out. And when, as she periodically does, Emma flips over into her pessimistic mode, suddenly very few people get hired. It's as if Emma imposes on her own a hiring freeze within the company.

She hates being in this position, and soon the manufacturing executives start harassing her with demands for new workers. Before long her optimism rules again.

She's on a dangerous path. As a decision maker, Emma's at risk of getting in trouble one too many times from being too optimistic. I've seen it happen before. Optimism leads to overextension, which leads to disaster, which leads to discouragement. One day the optimist falls down and can't get up. Who's more depressed than a pessimistic ex-optimist? But as you'll see, none of this is necessary.

The pessimist

Josh is just the opposite. He's a pessimist who constantly has failed flirtations with optimism. Josh too is a decision maker at work. He's a young development guy for a large independent-movie production company in Hollywood. He has projects dropped on his desk both from his bosses and from readers lower down in the organization. The notations all read in effect, "Can we do something with this?"

Josh's instinctive answer—his first answer, and all too often his last answer—is no. Here he is working in a town starving for good ideas, hell, for *any* ideas, and Josh sees disaster everywhere. There are always a hundred and one reasons why this project and that project can't be done right, and then more reasons why it will bomb even if it is done right.

Josh is clever. He always couches his memos in an "I'm just trying to save us from disaster here" style. A classic Josh memo: "This movie will not work without Gwyneth Paltrow. Gwyneth Paltrow will not do this movie. Therefore this movie will not work."

Remember what happened to Emma? The opposite happened to Josh. One day his boss, a well-known producer, called him into his office and said, "Look, if all we wanted was for projects to disappear down a black hole, we could send them to your office without you being there. We'd get the same result and it would be a lot cheaper."

So Josh felt the pressure to flip over into optimism, but it made him sick. He green-lighted projects that bombed because he couldn't balance his unaccustomed optimism with any note of caution. Soon, of course, Josh was lapsing back into pessimism.

This is what happens to all of us when we fall into one basic attitude or the other. We feel comfortable there, but every once in a while we're drawn to the other attitude. When that doesn't work, we fall back into our original attitude, thinking that because we've had more practice at it, it should work better, even if it doesn't.

Finding balance

People who make great choices ask, "Why do I have to be locked into one position or the other? It's actually easier and freer to take both positions at the same time."

The French philosopher Alain called this having optimism of the heart and pessimism of the intellect. In your heart, you hope for the best and expect the best. You know that good things are possible, and your heart leads you to search out ways good things can happen. Your heart is always looking for ways to turn lemons into lemonade.

Your head, without canceling out your heart, has well-learned knowledge of how things can go wrong. So your head leads you to search out likely disaster scenarios. Your head is looking for ways the glass of lemonade might fall off the table.

You have the right attitude when you have a balanced attitude. You're constantly hopeful, but you refuse to be blinded to what can go wrong.

Both Emma and Josh became aware of this law and tried to develop the right attitude. At first they were both afraid it wasn't even possible. But no one is either the Tin Man or the Scarecrow. We all have a heart and a brain. Use both.

Emma put together a plan. It was based on the idea that she could save her employers a lot of money if a greater percentage of new hires worked out. Now some of those savings were put into an employee development fund, to give extra help to at-risk new hires. Her bosses went for it. They could brag about this program in the community and gain valuable PR with the city.

Emma proved that hoping for the best and being prepared for the worst at the same time could create better decisions.

Josh got out of the business of red-lighting everything. Instead, he decided that about 10 percent of the projects that came his way had to be promising. Without making predictions about the future, Josh would keep looking for the best out of every ten projects. Then for each of these "best of ten" he created three lists.

- Risks [possible problems with the project].

- Needs [features the project would need to work].

- Opportunities [target markets, and ways this project could find these markets].

At first he was afraid he'd get in trouble for neither red-lighting nor green-lighting the projects he was forwarding. But his boss loved it. Josh was giving him a lot to work with and a lot to think about. By fully viewing the possible pluses and minuses, Josh could take credit for anything that turned out to be a success while having a record that would give him distance from anything that turned out to be a flop.

What both Josh and Emma discovered is one of the key reasons this law is so important. Information is the lifeblood of good decision making. Notice that by letting go of a purely optimistic or pessimistic stance, Josh and Emma developed procedures that generated more information than they'd had in the past. Josh created a wealth of new information about the projects he was reviewing, and Emma did the same with the new hires that had some risk attached to them.

The path of great decisions is paved with opportunity and prudence.

A balance of your own

How do you do what Josh and Emma did? Don't ask yourself if you're basically an optimist or a pessimist. Instead look back over some decisions you wish you'd made differently. How did you get into trouble? Were you consistently too optimistic or consistently too pessimistic?

If it's definitely one or the other, that's what you have to correct, but don't even try to go over to the other side. With every decision you face from now on, hold fast to your basic attitude, but then add to it information from the opposite stance.

If you've been too optimistic in the past, ask yourself, "Yeah, things might be great now, but how might they go wrong? What could I do to protect myself?" If you're always convinced you can leave for the airport at the last minute and still get there in time to make your flight, just think about traffic jams, for example, and let that influence your decision about when to leave. That's all it means to have a balanced attitude.

If you've been too pessimistic in the past, ask yourself, "What are some of the ways things could go right? What can I do to make sure I don't foreclose on the possibility of a pleasant surprise? What can I do to be ready if I am pleasantly surprised? And why not keep on trying to make things happen, even though I'm ready to be discouraged, because it's the only way good things have a chance?" Say yes to a blind date every now and then, wear clean underwear, and bring a condom. Why can't you let your heart say "maybe" even when your head says "no way"?

Having one and only one attitude puts you in danger. Naïve optimists make terrible choices. Pessimists either don't choose at all or make cramped, life-constricting choices. The people who make the best choices manage to cultivate simultaneously the basic expectation that things can and will turn out well with the ability to ask what can go wrong.

Law #13

Tune In to What You're Saying to Yourself

Have you remembered to really listen to yourself?

T HIS is the one law everyone knows, but often they know it too late. Sometimes I close my eyes and imagine a world full of people walking around, smacking themselves on the forehead, and saying, "Damn it, I should've listened to myself." The reality is not far from that. In one poll, 68 percent of people who made a bad choice said that before they made it they knew deep down that something was wrong.

It seems so easy. Just listen to yourself, and the road to great decisions lies shining before you.

But, as you know, if it really were that easy there wouldn't be all those people smacking themselves on the forehead. That's why you have to figure out how to listen to yourself. Here's how.

To really listen to yourself successfully, you need to know what to listen *for*. When I was a teenager, if I had problems with my car, my father would say, "What does the engine sound like?" I'd go out, listen, come back, and say, "What should I be listening for?" because I was basically clueless. There are special things good decision makers listen for, and I'll show you what they are.

What to listen for

There you are, facing the biggest decision of your life. Are you really going to quit your job and start a business? Are you really going to uproot your family and take them to work and live in Brazil? Are you really going to take all your savings and start actively investing in the stock market? Are you really going to go back to school?

A friend says, "This is a very big decision. Don't listen to other people. Listen to yourself."

So you listen and you listen and what you hear is . . . noise.

You're not alone. That's exactly why you and I don't listen to ourselves. It's not that we don't try. We try, but there's so much to hear that we get confused and end up saying to hell with it.

But the human capacity to sort through noise and tune in to what one really needs to hear is immense. My wife and I were once at my daughter's school for a parents' open-house night. I was in a classroom talking to one teacher. In the hallway throngs of people were walking back and forth. Suddenly, out of the countless confusing footsteps, I heard something and said, "That's my wife." The teacher couldn't believe it and neither could I when it turned out I was right.

So it's amazing what you can hear when you learn how to tune in. Now here you are facing a big decision. Here's what people who make good decisions *do* pay attention to when they listen to themselves:

→ *Listen to yourself saying, "It's what I've always wanted."*
Remember what you're looking for—that one choice, out of all the others, that will make you happy.

We get confused because there are lots of different kinds of positive things we say about our options. The mistake we make is to put them all on the same level. So we say, "This would be really smart." "If I don't do this now, I'll lose this great opportunity." "This will make a lot of other people happy." "If this works out, I'll get a lot out of it."

These are all positives. But how bankable are they? Some of these might be false or misleading. The world is full of clever schemes that seemed smart and turned bad.

Now suppose that out of all the different positive things you say to yourself about your different options, one thing you say is that this is an option you've always wanted. Nothing makes us happier than getting what we've always wanted. Getting something you've wanted for twenty years will make you happier than getting something you've wanted for one week. The fact that you've always wanted it is a kind of certificate of validity.

So if you listen and hear yourself saying "This is what I've always wanted" about one option, that's a strong indicator in favor of deciding on it.

→ *Listen to yourself saying, "This isn't good for me."*

If getting what you've always wanted is the gold standard of positivity, knowing something isn't good for you is the gold standard of negativity. We often have negative things in our heads when we're contemplating a major decision. Worries, what-ifs, assorted disaster scenarios, the sense that things are going to be tough.

If you listen to yourself without discernment, your nay-saying can paralyze you. For instance, when you're about to go swimming in the ocean. Or when your dance group is talking about giving a recital. Negative thoughts can plague us just as much when we're about to do something wonderful as when we're about to do something terrible.

Here is the one negativity you *should* listen to in yourself: the powerful feeling that the option you're about to choose won't be good for you.

A woman was thinking about embarking on a second marriage at age thirty-six. The guy was okay. In fact she enjoyed boasting about him to her friends. Still, it was a big decision and something held her back. She wrote down a list of pros and cons.

The pros went on and on. He had money. He liked her friends. He dressed well. Sex was great. They were both into skiing. His kids got along with her kids.

There was only one lonely con to offset all the pros. "I just don't think marriage is good for me." She was talking about having to coordinate her life with another person's needs and demands, and it made her feel hemmed in and angry. This was exactly the reason her first marriage had ended. A classic "I'm suffocating" scenario.

But she didn't listen to herself and got married anyway. It was a slow-motion disaster. Her discomfort and irritation made him angry, which made her sick, which held them both in a state of total misery. None of the pros on her list had mattered. Only the negative that pointed to her sense that this wouldn't be good for her. Don't do things you feel won't be good for you.

Of course, you should carefully examine your feeling that an option won't be good for you. Don't listen to yourself uncritically. Ask if there's a basis for this feeling. If there is, then this is a case where listening to yourself will save you from disaster.

You can immediately recognize the difference between the feeling that something won't be good for you and other forms of negativity that spin out of what-ifs. The mere possibility of trouble is not in itself a reason to turn away from a decision. But when you hear yourself say that something won't be good for you, you know that it's on a different level from fear of the unknown. You know yourself. You know how you've reacted to things in the past. If real experience tells you that something won't be good for you, *listen to that.*

➔ *Listen for what should be there but isn't.*
One of the best decision makers I interviewed for this book thought of this as the cornerstone of her ability to make good decisions. We all listen to ourselves. Most of us listen to what we're saying to ourselves. This woman listened to what she *wasn't* saying to herself that she *should* be saying.

Suppose you're hiring someone and you get a letter of recommendation about him. It will probably say something vaguely positive. But you're going to look for a note of enthusiasm, a note of praise of something specific. You should look for the same kind of thing inside yourself when you make a decision. The right kind of positive comments.

A hot young web designer had an idea for a new web-based e-commerce company. Pete was convinced he would join the ranks of millionaires with his idea—it was that good. But he wasn't sure he was ready. As he started thinking about launching his business he started listening to himself, and here's what he *didn't* hear.

He didn't hear a sense of confidence. He didn't hear a voice within saying, "I can do this."

There were many other voices inside him. Hope. Greed. Excitement. Dozens of good ideas. But not once did he hear himself say that he could do it.

Pete listened to himself and aborted the launch. He just sensed it was a mistake if he didn't feel utterly confident. Later he heard that a couple of his acquaintances started a similar business that crashed. Still, he wasn't sure he'd done the right thing. Three years later—an internet eternity—he got another idea. He liked this one just as much as he'd liked the first. There was a difference, though. This time he felt ready. He had a solidly based sense, when he listened to himself, that he could do it.

What he says is, "I hadn't realized how much of this business is about drumming up money from investors. That's why I think I wouldn't have been successful the first time. I believed in my idea, but I don't think I would've been successful in convincing them that I could carry it off. Why would they buy me when I hadn't bought myself? This time I'm sold on me. And it's funny because lots of times at meetings I don't know the answer to a question or I don't have a quick response to some negative comment. But that feeling I have, that I'm ready now, enables me to communicate confidence. They're buying me because they can sense that I've bought myself."

If you're about to make a decision, ask yourself what you should be saying to yourself with this kind of decision. Don't be afraid to go with the obvious. For example, if you're about to commit to spending your life with someone, you should be saying to yourself how happy you are and how this feels right to you. Will you have doubts? Sure. But if you also hear what you should be hearing, that's an important plus. Not hearing it is a major reason to say no.

To take another example, if you're about to embark on a major enterprise like Pete's, you should be hearing yourself say, "I'm ready. I have everything I need to go forward now."

Suppose you're deciding to leave one situation and enter another—changing jobs, for example. You should be hearing within yourself a lot of confident talk about how the new situation is solidly and significantly better than the old one. If you're thinking of changing jobs and you're not telling yourself how the new job is a big improvement, maybe you're just playing musical chairs.

You be the judge. Whatever big decision you're facing, ask what you should be saying to yourself about it. When you listen to yourself, is that what you hear?

→ *Listen for yourself saying the same thing over and over.*

Listening to yourself is a process. If some hope or fear comes into your head, you probably chew on it and check it out. That's why the things we say to ourselves when we face a decision don't stay the same. They ebb and flow, appear and disappear.

Maybe you're thinking of buying a boat. There was a point at which you thought about how expensive it was, but then expense stopped coming up as an issue. For some reason you took care of that. One thought stays constant, however. You keep saying to yourself, "But how often will we use it?" That concern never leaves you.

Well, listen carefully to what you're saying to yourself. Sometimes we don't give weight to something we say to ourselves because we've heard it before. We treat ourselves like a nagging parent. When it comes to listening to yourself, it should be the opposite. The more often you say something to yourself, the more weight you should give it.

→ *Listen to yourself say, "This is me," or "This isn't me."*

What are you more of an expert on than anything else? You're an expert on you. Let's say you own a successful restaurant and you come up with the idea of turning your one location into a chain. You have a good concept and you think it will fly. All you'll have to do is open another one annually until the momentum picks up and you can become a full-fledged franchiser.

You can pull in dozens of experts to help you decide about the process of opening a new restaurant. But what about you? How do you fit into the equation? There are two things you might be saying to yourself.

"This is me," meaning that this decision really fits what you know about who you are and how you work and what makes you happy and what brings out the best in you.

Or "This isn't me," meaning that this decision might be a good decision for a dozen different reasons, and it might be a wonderful opportunity for someone else, but it doesn't fit what you know about who you are and how you work and what makes you happy and what brings out the best in you.

The trick here is to be honest about what it means "to be me." Maybe you enjoy seeing yourself sitting behind a big desk at the head of a gigantic enterprise surrounded by a swarm of sycophantic assistants. Maybe you get excited at the thought of having a ton of cash.

But life is what you live, not what you have. "This is me" is all about what suits the way you actually function best, and the way you enjoy functioning, not about what you'd get if your dream came true. So when you think about a decision, you have to think about living that decision minute by minute, in your skin, with your feelings and tastes and nerves.

Just think about all the people who want to be writers. What most of them really want is *to have written*. But deciding to write is about deciding to live a solitary existence, with no one to pace or motivate you besides yourself. That's what you think about when you ask yourself, "Is this me or not?"—the inescapable everydayness of living out your decision.

When you're torn

What do you do if you try to listen to yourself and you hear two very different things? A woman who was thinking of becoming a candidate for a major project at work heard one voice inside her say, "What are you waiting for? This is a really good opportunity. You know a lot." Another voice said, "I don't feel ready."

How do you decide which voice to listen to?

One thing to look for is intensity. If one voice is accompanied with flop sweats and nausea and the other isn't, you pay attention to the first voice.

Another thing to look for is the wagging finger. One voice is telling you who you should be. The other voice is telling you who you are. Pay attention to the voice that's telling you who you are. Decisions that are made based on who you think you should be are great, but they work only when who you should be matches who you really are. If these don't match, you won't be successful if you decide based on who you should be.

If you're torn when you try to listen to yourself, *both* voices together may really be telling you that you're not ready to decide. You need to check things out more carefully and get better prepared. Then you'll find that one of the voices goes away.

We're all in danger of falling into what I call the *low-self-trust trap.* That happens when you've made some bad decisions or you're scared of a big new decision and you stop listening to yourself because you don't trust yourself. The trap appears when the less you trust yourself, the less you listen to yourself. The less you listen to yourself, the worse your decisions are. The worse your decisions are, the less you trust yourself.

The good news is that this can be completely reversed. But don't even try to begin by trusting yourself. Begin by listening to yourself. Then you will make good decisions. Then you will feel more self-trust. Then trusting yourself will come automatically.

If you want to make good decisions, stop judging yourself and start listening to yourself.

Law #14

Never Let a Lower Priority Outweigh a Higher Priority

Are your priorities all out of whack?

O F the thirty laws, this may be the one that's violated most often. I almost violated this law by not including it as a chapter.

I was thinking that it's important to present this decision-making guide in a highly accessible way, and a discussion of priorities might be indigestible, particularly since most of us have a hard time struggling to find out what our priorities are. But a much higher priority for me was to offer the actual laws followed by people who make great choices. So I was saved at the last minute from making a bad decision because I remembered this law. Some of us aren't so lucky.

Getting your priorities straight

Carly owned a lamp store in Manhattan with her husband, Al. When they first started, they opened a store on the Lower East Side near Orchard Street. Al fell in love with the layout because it was big for the rent they'd have to pay. They got a bargain on all that space because the store wasn't on a main shopping thorough-fare. That was a legitimate priority for someone just starting out: get a nice big store. But how much does size matter? Is having the biggest store actually a high priority?

Carly soon saw that they were making a bad decision by stay-ing there. There was a lamp district on the Bowery, a few blocks over. People from all five boroughs who needed lamps—householders, decorators, landlords, and so on—went to the Bowery to shop. They wouldn't wander down to Carly and Al's store in a million years. So what good was it to have a big store when you didn't have customers to fill it? They just weren't turning over the merchandise.

Carly's family had been in the lamp business, and she was confident about her ability to stock and sell good lamps. But none of that could happen without customers walking in off the street. Carly begged Al to move. But when Al saw what the rents were in the lamp district for a store that size he wouldn't budge. "Al, what good is so much space if you don't have customers?" Carly said.

This story finally had a happy ending. Carly was wise enough to persist. Behind Al's back she kept her eyes open for a store in the lamp district that she could rent for not that much more than they were paying. When a good deal on a small store turned up, she twisted Al's arm and he agreed. They made a lot more money in the smaller store because three times as many people came in. The sad part is that they wasted ten years because of Al's fixation on the much lower priority of having a "big store."

You can see how easy it is to violate this law. A priority hangs in front of you like a shining star. It absorbs you. Maybe it obsesses you. And here's where we *really* get into jeopardy: This priority you're focusing on is absolutely valid in and of itself. So you treat it as if it were one of the Ten Commandments—something absolutely and utterly inviolable.

In the real world, we all have a bunch of priorities. Typically they're all valid, but they all point in different directions when it comes to providing guidance about your decision. You can almost never do justice to all your priorities. And frankly it's tough to come up with a perfect ranking of different priorities.

What you can do—what you must do—is make sure you never, ever make a decision based on a much lower priority while ignoring another option that would satisfy a much higher priority.

That's the work of decision making. You can't short-circuit this work by hanging on to one priority and giving it an importance it doesn't have.

Ask yourself what your priorities should be. Make every decision—big or little, simple or complicated—by choosing an option that best does justice to your priorities roughly in the order you rank them. That's the critical issue here: will you make sure that you never, ever give a lower priority more weight than a higher priority?

Of course we all want to say yes. No one starts out determined to let a lower priority trump a higher priority. So how does it happen that we do the one thing we wouldn't want to do? Remember Al, who fell in love with his "big store"? Al got in trouble because he got distracted.

Overcoming distraction

I was once driving along with the windows open and a bee flew in the car. I panicked. I let go of the wheel, waved my hands around, and started looking at the bee, not the road. I'm lucky I didn't get into a major accident, because I was going over fifty down a twisting two-lane country road.

That's exactly how we end up violating this law. Acting in accordance with your priorities is as intuitive as driving down a road. What could be easier? But then a bee gets in your car.

That's the key to making sure you never violate this law. Identify the buzzing bees that are preventing you from keeping your eyes on the road. Here are the big ones.

➜ *Immediate gratification.*
The possibility of a bit of satisfaction today is one bee that distracts you from the possibility of a lot of satisfaction tomorrow.

I knew a guy who'd been struggling along as a writer. He got published, but his literary novels didn't earn him any money. His wife was threatening to kick him out, and he saw that if he didn't start a new career now while he was still in his thirties, it would only be a lot harder later. The decision was whether to stop cold or do one more book.

Every sign pointed to stopping cold. There was no indication from anyone, including his publisher and editor, that his new book would earn him more money than he'd make as a clerk at Barnes & Noble. But this guy had gotten a bee in his bonnet: He'd heard about voice-recognition software with which you could "talk" instead of type your book and there'd be fewer errors than if you had typed it. He was very excited about the possibility of using that software. It seemed fun and cool, and he had a vague sense that talking a novel might make it better, or at least faster.

So he decided to write one more novel. The basis for that decision was the extremely low-level priority of being able to play with voice-recognition software. The prospect of immediate gratification distracted him from seeing that his life was in an emergency state.

His wife left him. The book made no more money than his previous books. Yet this bad decision was no different from a million bad decisions people make every day. They're all the same: some bee gets in our bonnet and distracts us from our higher priorities.

Some of the deepest and most important decisions can be threatened by the "bee" of immediate gratification. Even affairs of state. Take the Cuban Missile Crisis back in the 1960s. Was President Kennedy a bad decision maker because he risked war over those missiles?

We have detailed evidence of the discussions that went into Kennedy's decision. It was a great decision—not because Khrushchev backed down, but because Kennedy understood how unlikely it was that Khrushchev would bring on World War III just to keep a few missiles in Cuba. For Kennedy, immediate gratification would have come by letting Khruschev have his way and keep missiles in Cuba, just to avoid the threat of war. But as gratifying as that might be, Kennedy saw there was a higher priority. The higher priority was to avoid a precedent in which Soviet strategic arms could threaten the United States in our own hemisphere, where there would be almost no warning of an attack.

Undergoing a little risk today to get greater security in the future generally makes sense, but only if you can see past what you're giving up today and appreciate what you'll get tomorrow.

Look back over your own bad decisions. You'll see an amazing number of cases where you opted for a little satisfaction today and didn't think about the future satisfaction you were giving up.

Think about a decision you're facing now. Maybe you're thinking about getting a new job. If you're like most of us the mere thought of looking for a job makes you want to pull the covers over your head and take a nap. It takes a lot of heartache and shoe leather to look for a job, and a lot of time is time you don't have.

Job satisfaction may be the single most important ingredient in life satisfaction. How can you love your life if you hate the place where you spend most of your life? Yet we stick around in jobs we hate, buying decades of unhappiness for the price of some briefly gratifying stress reduction today. That's an example of how some "bee" has flown in and distracted us from a much higher priority.

→ *Urgency.*

Another "bee" is the buzz of urgency. Every time we do what's urgent instead of what's important we violate this law.

Let's look at some of the ways urgency creeps in to distract us from a much higher priority. Suppose, for example, you have someone in your life—a boss, a spouse, a relative, a friend—who has not the slightest compunction about raising a ruckus when he or she wants something. There are things that are important to you in your life, but this person manages to trump the higher priority of the things that are really important to you with the lower priorities they're focused on. You get distracted by the urgency of *their* priorities.

Let's talk about impulsiveness—that's just another form of urgency. Bad decision makers tend to be impulsive decision makers. What about good decision makers? I can tell you from personal experience that they have the same impulses that everyone else does. When the bee flies into your car you've got to deal with the bee in your car. But good decision makers don't let the urgency of their impulses rule their priorities.

Let's say you're in graduate school. You have an old, unreliable car and not much money. One evening while you're driving home it breaks down again. You blow up. Leaving your car by the side of the road you walk into a dealership across the way and sign up for a brand-new car that's a lot more than you can afford. You had a problem and you had to do something. But the pinprick of frustration combined with the accident of opportunity led you to do something that wasn't good for you. Saving money so you can stay in school is a higher priority than having a new car.

Notice how easy it is to get your priorities thrown out of whack. Something happens—your car breaks down, or you don't have much money to pay rent for a store, or an enemy of the country threatens war. You're misled because, like a bee, this priority becomes so utterly urgent that you don't even stop to think whether another priority comes first.

So do this. Look back on a bad decision. What were your priorities when you made that decision? What should your priorities have been? Notice how you substituted a lower priority for a higher priority as a reason for making your decision.

Think of some big decision you're facing now. You're tempted to make that decision in a certain way because of a priority. What is that priority?

Now give yourself the opportunity to take one step toward your life the way you would like it to be. Say to yourself, "This priority I've been making such a big deal of may be important. But is there a priority that's more important and that should carry more weight?"

Trust yourself to come up with the correct answer to that question. You will answer it correctly if you remember to ask it and if you give yourself breathing room to answer it according to the truth of what you know about yourself and your world. Be particularly on the lookout for the forces in your life—the need for immediate gratification and the pressures of urgency—that are distracting you from your top priorities.

Good decisions are born in a moment of stillness and silence. We're all distracted by pressures of one sort or another. But if you can find that still place where you can see what's pushing you in one direction and then see if there's some other force you should be paying more attention to, you'll never get distracted to the point where you let a low priority rule.

Perspectives

Knowing Your Priorities

W HAT *are* your priorities, anyway?
When asked this question, most of us will talk in vague
generalities—family, happiness, caring for others, success. That's no
good. These are no more guides to action than being told you can
find someone's house by "going north." If "family" is a priority and
you're offered a job far away where your kids will be far from their
grandparents, do you take it? Who knows? With vague priorities you
can justify anything. Saying "I never want to live more than an hour
away from my extended family"—now that's a priority. Any clear and
powerful guide to action is a real priority. Then the only question is
whether it's actually your priority.

So how do you come up with something solid and specific you
can actually use?

Here's what you do. Ask yourself four questions:

- What do I like?

- What do I need?

- What am I good at?

- What's threatening me?

You can ask these questions about yourself and your life
in general, or about aspects of your life, like your career or your

relationship. It's best to come up with many answers to each question.

Then you have to get tough with yourself. No matter how many answers you come up with, force yourself to pare down the list. Do this until you have no more than three answers to each question. Four questions, three answers each—that makes twelve priorities.

Now write out each of these priorities as an affirmative statement of what you need to do or what's important to you. For example: "I've got to start saving a lot of money for my retirement." "I need to find work that I like." "I've got to kick my career into high gear." "This next period of my life is when I have to start a business." "I've got to make my marriage work." "I've got to figure out why I've been feeling so poorly and do something about it."

I'm not saying any of these should be your priority. I'm just saying that you want to come up with statements as simple, solid, specific, and direct as these.

Now you have twelve, but that's still too many. Most people find that three priorities are all they can handle. So look at your list and say, "If I had to eliminate one which would I eliminate?" Then draw a line through it.

Now draw a line through your next least important priority. And the next one. And the next one. Keep doing this, difficult as it is, until you get down to three priorities.

You were saying you don't know what your priorities are? Look at those three. They're your top three priorities.

Never again in your life will you make better use of your time than in listing your top three priorities. You'll be simplifying your life and you'll be discovering what you really need.

These top three priorities are it—never let any other priority have more weight.

Law #15

No Matter What, Don't Get Trapped

Are you protecting yourself from getting stuck?

M AKING bad decisions sucks. People who make bad choices not only end up in a worse place, they also find that they've made it harder for themselves to make good decisions in the future. That's because bad decisions bring you to a place where you have fewer, worse options.

That's pretty bad, but it's not the worst thing that can happen to you. The real horror is falling into a trap. What I mean by that is falling into a place where you're almost literally stuck, unable to move, unable to save yourself. Trying to jump over a log and spraining your ankle—maybe that was a bad decision. But you get over it. Falling into quicksand—that's a trap.

People who make great decisions make their share of bad decisions; no one's perfect. But they fight like hell to make sure they never get stuck in a trap.

The issue of traps and how to avoid them is critical. Once you understand it, your life will change.

A trap in action

Here's a perfect illustration of how we fall into traps in life.

Let's say you're in a city and you want to go somewhere that would take you a good thirty minutes to walk. You decide to take a bus that should get you there in five minutes. You start waiting for the bus. The next thing you know, twenty minutes have gone by, and still no bus. Now what do you do?

If you're like a lot of people, you say, "I've waited this long, I'll feel stupid if I start walking now and suddenly the bus comes." So, restless and impatient, you keep waiting.

This is where most people fall into a trap. Because you've waited so long, you've invested in waiting. You've made a commitment to waiting. And so waiting begets more waiting. You come up with reasons: "The longer I've waited, the more likely it is that the bus will show up any second." So you keep waiting, making it even more likely (you think) that the bus will show up.

You're in a trap. You're always in a trap when the more you do something, the more you feel you have to keep on doing it.

People fall into traps at every turn. Entire nations fall into traps. The United States got trapped in Vietnam. We had sacrificed so many men and so many dollars, how could we not keep fighting? So we sacrificed more men and more dollars. After the first sacrifice of men and dollars, the administration believed it had to be that much closer to victory. This was the famous "light at the end of the tunnel" everyone thought they saw.

On a more personal level, we get trapped like this in bad relationships. You give so much time and energy to someone else that if things still aren't very good, you keep hanging in there because of how much hanging in there you've done already.

We get trapped like this in bad business ventures. A guy I know has been slowly bleeding to death—emotionally and financially— as the owner of a small music store in Boston. Now, Boston's not a bad town for a music store; it has lots of musicians and lots of student musicians. But there are a lot of music stores. This guy hangs in there year after year, working long hours, facing endless staff turnover, problems with suppliers, fears about losing customers and gaining competitors, and he makes just enough money to keep him trapped in hope. He told me, "I *wish* something would happen so I'd go bankrupt. Then this would be over. I've put in so much time already, I just keep thinking I'll turn a corner one day and figure out a way to actually make a decent living from this."

He's still waiting.

This kind of trap is known to experts as a source of fatal flying accidents. You leave an airport where the weather's good and fly toward an area where, it turns out, the weather's bad, but not so bad that you're forced to turn around. So you think, "Well, I've flown this far already, and it's a long way back to where I started from, and I'm not that far from where I want to go, so let me fly for another five minutes and see what happens."

Every year pilots die because this psychological trap prevents them from making a U-turn.

How we trap ourselves

Now you see why traps like this are so important. They're as seductive as a hundred-dollar bill lying on a deserted sidewalk. As tough to deal with as a hundred-dollar bill that's been glued to the sidewalk. Here are the ways traps play a role in decision making:

→ *Things look so promising that you think you don't have any choice.*

Los Angeles, New York, and some other big cities are filled with people trying to make it in the entertainment business. Many of them have absolutely no talent, get nowhere fast, and quickly get the point that they'd better do something less risky and more rewarding. They're the lucky ones.

If they're incredibly *un*lucky, they have reason to believe they have promise. Someone, somewhere encouraged them. They read about how Madonna auditioned for the TV show *Fame* and didn't make it, and they think, "Well, I have so much to offer, I know I too will click if I just hang in there."

But it's the same as the guy waiting for the bus, or the person in the lousy relationship: hanging in there just digs you in to a situation in which you believe you have to keep on hanging in there.

We're encouraged from the time we're children to look for those slow, steady bits of evidence that we're making progress. You get on the diving board and try to do a back flip. The first few times it's hopeless. Then your father says, "You're starting to get it."

Then he says, "That time you almost got it." Who's going to stop working on her back flips at that point?

To get out of traps, we have to be able to see when "promise" is just an empty promise.

→ *You've invested so much in a particular choice that it just seems crazy not to keep on investing in it.*
Decision making is all about figuring out what is the best thing to do. What shoes are you going to wear tomorrow? The best decision is to wear the shoes that make the most sense. But suppose that for whatever crazy reason you'd fallen in love with clogs, and now you have a closet full of them. If you've fallen into this psychological trap, you'll go with the clogs.

That's a mistake. The best decision is *still* to wear the shoes that make the most sense. Who cares how many clogs you've invested in?

A doctor I know is one of the world's unhappiest men. After graduating from a super-prestigious medical school and completing a long residency in anesthesiology, he realized that practicing medicine was boring and generally frustrating and annoying. That was twenty years ago. But he'd invested so much in becoming a doctor. That investment prevented him from seeing his real choices. He should've asked himself, "What's the best thing for me, a talented man, to do with the rest of my life, regardless of what I've done with my life so far?"

Instead, he ended up wasting his life.

This is what traps make us do. We stay there because we're seduced into thinking it's incredibly reasonable to be there.

How to never, ever be trapped

Avoiding traps requires discipline. I'm talking about the kind of discipline that makes it possible for you to set a limit or boundary, and when that's crossed you just turn around and walk away.

Here's how to avoid traps and escape them if you should happen to fall in.

→ **Don't confuse situations where persistence is a virtue with situations where persistence is part of being trapped.**

Persistence *is* a virtue, but only when it makes sense. It makes sense only when specific evidence shows that the cost of persisting is small compared to the possible gain.

The guy with the struggling music store—what evidence did he have that things would ever be better? None. The guy who hated being a doctor—what day-to-day experiences ever gave him the sense that he would start loving it? None. These are clearly people who were persisting for no reason.

So don't persist unless the costs are small compared to the possible benefits. Make sure the possible benefits are real. And make sure they're highly likely.

→ **Set goals and deadlines.**

To show how this works, let's go back to the person waiting for the bus. You show up at the bus stop, knowing that walking takes half an hour and a trip on the bus takes five minutes. You're not sure how often the buses come. How do you prevent yourself from getting stuck waiting?

You pick a deadline where you'll stop waiting and start walking. Ten minutes, twenty minutes; it doesn't matter. The winners aren't the ones who pick the best deadline. The winners are the ones who pick *some* deadline and stick to it.

That's why getting out of traps requires discipline. You have to be able to show up at the bus stop, say to yourself you'll start walking if the bus hasn't come in ten minutes, and then if the bus hasn't come by then, start walking no matter what.

This applies everywhere. Let's say you just started a new job, and now that you're there you realize you hate it. You are immediately at risk of falling into a terrible trap. Every day you stay in a job you hate is a day you've invested, and as the investments mount you'll find it harder and harder to leave. So you set a goal and a deadline. Again, don't worry about whether the goal and the deadline are brilliant and perfect. Worry about being tough enough to act if the goal hasn't been met once you reach the deadline.

For example, you might say, "This should be a really good job.

So there's no reason to leave it immediately. But I'm going to give myself one year to the day. If by that time I don't have a promotion or I can't say I'm enjoying the job more days than not, then I'm immediately launching a full-scale search for a new job."

That's how people who make good choices stay out of traps. When Carleton Fiorina was made CEO of Hewlett-Packard, she became the first woman to head a Fortune 100 company. She is obviously someone who makes good choices. Here's how she got out of a potential trap. Right out of Stanford she went to law school. She soon realized that she didn't like it. Did she stay stuck? No. As soon as it was clear that law wasn't for her, she just left right in the middle of her studies.

Unusual? Not for good decision makers. Lawyers have among the lowest job and career satisfaction among any occupation, professional or otherwise. There are a lot of lawyers who saw at some point that they were unhappy, but they didn't leave. They'd pinned their hopes on being lawyers, after all. They'd worked so hard in law school, investing both time and money. But they didn't set a goal or a deadline when the first sign of unhappiness set in, or if they did, they didn't act on it. Carly Fiorina did. And she got free.

→ *Understand that bygones are bygones—today is the first day of the rest of your life.*
Writers are people who make decisions too. They decide what to write, word by word. And with every word a writer writes, he's creating an investment.

Bad writers get stuck because they're fixated on the intellectual and emotional investment they've made in the words they've put on paper. Good writers write crap just the same as bad writers. But then they make good decisions about their writing.

For example, the late Nobel Prize winner Isaac Bashevis Singer, a family friend and a very sweet person, was a firm believer in letting yourself fly free during the creative process. Once that was finished, however, he was ruthless toward his own words. No matter how many tears or how much blood he shed to set a scene, if it didn't serve the story, it was gone. What he'd invested of himself in the writing was nothing. What he was trying to accomplish was everything. He never kept a word in simply because it had taken him trouble to put in that word.

Take John Updike as another example. He has said he throws away one book he writes for every book he actually publishes. Who cares how much time he put into writing it? It's sad to let go of an investment of months. But people who make good decisions understand that the value of an investment is what it's worth now, not how much you've put into it, and they're willing to cut their losses.

Smart Wall Street investors say the same thing. You buy a stock for a lot of money and it goes down and you lose confidence in it? Sell without delay. Winners aren't afraid to sell when they buy a loser. That's because they understand that falling into a trap is always worse than losing a few bucks.

→ *Always and continually give yourself options and alternatives.* One of the facets of getting trapped is cutting yourself off from other possibilities. The longer you stay in a bad relationship, the harder it is to go to your little black book and have people to call to get back into circulation. The longer you stay in a job that isn't right for you, the more opportunities you lose to demonstrate your excellence.

Whether it's your job, your career, your relationship, or your investments, it's always worth asking yourself, "What else could I be doing instead of this?"

People who make great decisions understand that there are always other possibilities. And if things are iffy, they make sure they know what those possibilities are.

Don't be afraid to cut your losses. Don't be afraid to switch direction. Don't be afraid to make new things happen. And don't be afraid of failure. Everyone fails and gets into trouble at some point, including people who make great decisions. But good decision makers understand that nothing, absolutely nothing, is more important than holding on to the freedom to make choices. That's what it means to stay out of traps.

Law #16

Know Your Achilles' Heel

What are the top ten bad habits in making decisions?

A CHILLES had two heels but only one Achilles' heel. Actually, that's important. We're all far from perfect, particularly when it comes to making big decisions. But with all your little imperfections, if you know your biggest bad habit, you'll put yourself in the class of people who make great choices.

For example, I know how to eat so I stay at my healthiest weight. But I have a weakness: postponing meals during the day, snacking when I'm hungry, and then eating a big meal late at night. Knowing my weakness is good. If I can make sure to eat during the day so I'm not hungry at night, then I've protected myself.

And so it is with making decisions. All of us are filled with weaknesses and imperfections. So how do you become someone who always makes great decisions?

Identify your biggest bad decision habit, and work at not making that one specific error. You'll be amazed at how much better a decision maker you become by trying to avoid just that one biggest weakness.

Get that shoehorn away from me

Think about two decisions in your life:

- The last big decision you made.

- The worst decision you ever made.

Now think about what was in your mind and in your heart when you made them.

The following is a list of the ten biggest, most common bad decision habits. Ask yourself which of these bad habits played the biggest role in your decisions. You'd be surprised at how accurately we know ourselves when it comes to making decisions. Trust yourself to recognize your biggest bad decision habit when you read about it.

#1. Biting off more than you can chew

Have you ever cleaned up after a dinner party and tried to carry more dishes in one trip than you could handle, only to have everything come crashing down? That's what happens when we bite off more than we can chew.

It's easy to identify this bad decision habit. The word "enough" feels horribly wrong to you. You feel personally challenged by it. Enough? No! You must have more! A lower ambition is not as good as a higher ambition. Doing things the easy way is not as good as doing things the hard way. Doing fewer things is not as good as doing more things.

Of course we don't say, "I'm biting off more than I can chew." Instead we talk about what high standards we have, how we have a right to expect the best, how we work so hard and have so much to offer that we deserve good things.

One sign that overreaching has raised its ugly head is hearing yourself say, "I don't care if it's not realistic, I know what I want." But over and over you have the feeling that the whole huge, shaky pile is collapsing around you. You collapse from exhaustion. You fail at basic responsibilities. You make everyone angry and disappointed with you at the same time. You keep falling behind as a result of trying to move ahead.

#2. Detail mania

Every once in a while some little detail you overlook gets you in serious trouble. That's why it's so easy for many of us to get paranoid and start worrying a lot about details. Many professionals—from doctors to airplane mechanics, from systems analysts to paralegals—must deal with details, and many of us are one step away from falling victim to detail mania.

"Detail mania" is just another name for irrelevancy overload. All it does is slow you down and make it incredibly difficult for you to see the forest for the trees. Detail mania leads to bad decisions because it prevents you from focusing on what's most important.

If you take a lot of pride in your attention to detail, watch out. If the high point of your day is catching someone when they screw up on some detail, watch out. If you're convinced that the details are what's most important, watch out. We're never so vulnerable to any bad habit as when we take pride in it.

#3. Fear

You could be deciding anything—whether to marry someone, whether to change jobs, whether to let yourself accept a nomination to be Chairman of the Joint Chiefs of Staff—and what guides you most is what you're most afraid might happen. That's what this weakness is all about.

Don't misunderstand me. We sometimes have to make a decision because we feel threatened. You're working on the job and you hear rumors that your company is being bought by another company. You decide to search for a new job. Fear got you going.

Fear becomes a bad habit, however, when it plays an exaggerated role in your decision-making process.

The most common exaggerated fear is that you'll make a mistake. The second is the fear of making other people mad at you. And the third is fear of some huge catastrophe that might come along if you make a certain choice.

If fears like these paralyze you or prevent you from making a good choice, this is your bad decision habit.

With this bad habit, as with all the others, one of the signs you've got the habit is how proud you are of it. Of course, you wouldn't call it being fearful. You'd call it being cautious. But be honest with yourself: if you're motivated mainly by fear of loss rather than hope of gain, then fear, not prudence, is ruling.

#4. Losing touch with you

You've got this bad decision habit if your decision depends on listening too much to other people, following other people, and trying to please other people. Frank Sinatra said, "I did it my way." You'd say, "I did it his way."

This is a very understandable bad habit. After all, we're talking about those big decisions where you're wandering through murky territory with something important at stake. People who are lost want to follow a leader. Of course it's good to consult experts and get input from other people. But people who have this bad habit don't get input from *themselves*.

Here's one way you know you have this bad habit. When someone asks you why you did something, you're likely to say that it was because someone advised you or because you listened to someone or because someone pressured you.

You have to watch out for losing touch with yourself if the desire to please someone else makes it hard for you to give full weight to, or to even see, what you really want.

#5. The green-eyed monster

You've got this bad habit if you want what someone else has got. In other words, your lifestyle was okay until you got a glimpse of someone else's lifestyle. Your children were doing fine until you saw how someone else's children were doing. You were content with the money you were making until you saw how much money someone else was making.

Envy is a bad habit because it pulls you out of yourself and infects your ability to make smart choices. At work, for example, you leave the areas you're good at and start working areas someone else is good at. You lose sight of what you really want because you're so obsessed with wanting what someone else has.

It's just a fact that people who make great decisions stay within the orbit of what works for them, of what they're good at, of what they need. Crucially, they can say, "Yes, that may be right for you, but it's not right for me."

#6. Keeping on keeping on

You've got this bad habit if you keep going along the way you've been going along—why rock the boat? Someone who can't leave a bad relationship or a bad job because he's used to staying and because change is hard has this bad habit. (By the way, don't confuse this bad habit with simply doing nothing.)

Keeping on is also a problem for people who impulsively start the ball rolling toward a decision, then don't feel they can stop it or change its direction. For example, if you start a new business and believe you can't change direction as new information comes your way, you're caught in this bad habit.

People who make great decisions don't let themselves get caught up in momentum. They're ready to change direction at any time.

#7. Acting without thinking

You've got this bad decision habit if you frequently make decisions without stopping, looking, listening, weighing, thinking, thinking some more, and then finally acting. Over and over again you look back at your decisions and say, "What was I thinking?"

But if you always remember the following three guidelines, based on laws you've already read, you'll never be caught acting without thinking.

- First, *remember to ask yourself how things will play out over time.* Say you're on special medication and you go away for a few days. Suddenly you have the option of staying a couple more days, but you can't because you didn't bring extra medication. In the beginning you should've said to yourself, "You know, there's always the possibility that I'll be staying longer, so is there anything I should bring, just in case?" You look ahead down the road when you're driving, and there's no reason you can't do that when you're making a decision.

- Second, *remember what your priorities are.* Every guy who ever destroyed a marriage because he fooled around is a guy who completely lost sight of his priorities. How much thinking does it take to just stop and ask yourself what your priorities are?

- Third, *remember to take care of yourself.* Let's say you have a good job but a bad boss. You decide to stay because the money is good enough and you vaguely hope things will get better. That's not taking care of yourself. A bad boss will change the environment for the worse and take you down with it. The minute you find yourself with a bad boss, you have to take care of yourself and start looking for a new job, making sure also that you document everything you've done, particularly your accomplishments, in case your boss should somehow try to undermine your career.

#8. Dithering

One of the bad decision habits is *dithering.* This involves staying undecided *way* past your need to make a decision.

Chip was a ditherer. He had made a name for himself as a director of TV commercials, but his dithering almost destroyed everything he'd built.

His dithering was not a problem in his early career. There was never enough money at stake when he did low-budget productions to cause a problem.

It's when Chip entered the big leagues that he started getting in trouble. One time Chip arrived on location to do a perfume ad. He got the job because he had a reputation for making good choices when it came to shooting commercials. But Chip couldn't settle on one clear vision for the ad. Should it be sexy? More romantic? More exotic? A one-day shoot turned into a three-day shoot at five times the money.

By dithering Chip spent three days chasing after what amounted to a slight improvement over the original concept, while royally upsetting the people who'd hired him. His bad habit was turning a fine commercial filmmaker into an unemployable one.

When Chip got fired he went, in despair, to his mentor, a famous and highly respected Hollywood director whom he had worked for as an assistant out of film school.

His mentor told Chip something very smart. "All my best movies will never be made. They're still in my head. Making a *good* movie isn't about searching until you've found what you're looking for. It's about working fast. If you have a vision, it will come through. If you don't have a vision, nothing will save you, certainly not spending days trying to make up your mind."

Chip was astounded. Part of him had taken pride in dithering, as if that's what great artists did. Now he knew to cut it out.

Dithering begins when the cost of not deciding one way or the other starts to outweigh the benefits of continuing to check things out. In other words, think of the time you spend making a decision *as an investment*. At the beginning you get a great return on your investment. Fairly soon the return starts to flatten out; before you know it, it's costing you.

Imagine you're going to a restaurant with some friends. Obviously you're going to want to look at the menu before you order. So far you're getting a return on the time you're spending. You might want to spend a little time thinking about a couple of top options. That's fine too. But when you start dragging out your lunch hour, irritating people, you're dithering.

The minute you start fiddling with changes that probably don't make much difference or that can easily be fixed later, you're dithering.

#9. Taking the path of least resistance

You've got this bad habit if you hate taking the time and trouble to look into things. As far as you're concerned the best decision is the one you can make the fastest and easiest. Instead of searching for the right ad agency for your firm, you'll go with one that has offices in your building. Or a friend's ad agency. Or the first agency recommended to you.

Looking for a job? You'll take the first halfway decent job that's offered to you, because you hate looking for jobs.

You don't think of yourself as lazy so much as efficient. You take pride in how fast you make decisions. You like seeing yourself as rough and ready, grab and go. You have stories of how you went shopping for an important garment, grabbed the first decent thing you saw, and walked out of the store in a mere fifteen minutes. (And I know someone reading these words is saying, "Hell, I was done in five minutes.") The idea of taking the time to search for some wonderful options makes you antsy, almost scared.

#10. Not believing that things can be better than they are

You've got this bad habit if you're down on hope. You may not feel depressed, but when the possibility of change presents itself, it's very hard for you to see how there could be improvement.

When you first look at the possibility of change, you might say, "But if I do that, all that will happen is . . ." and then you reel off a list of bad outcomes you're sure to see. When you're caught in it, it doesn't feel like negativity, it feels like realism. In fact, you take pride in seeing ahead to all the ways good things can't happen.

This is a particularly dangerous bad decision habit. Being so aware of how things can go wrong, you're supercautious. If opportunity knocks, you don't throw yourself into its arms, and so you create a self-fulfilling prophecy.

Do you recognize any of these ten bad decision habits in yourself? If so, you're safe as long as you remember to say, "Here I go again. I know how I keep getting in trouble. Let me stay out of that trouble this time."

Be particularly aware of the ways you boast of your bad habits. Don't believe that boast. It's like that friend you had in high school who kept getting you into trouble. Stay away.

Bad habits get us into trouble and are hard to overcome, but people who make great decisions try to avoid them. There's an old expression: fore-warned is forearmed. This is never truer than when it comes to your biggest bad habits in making decisions.

Law #17

Always Take Your Own Best Advice

Would you tell your best friend to do this?

W E use the Golden Rule of "Do unto others . . ." all the time in our lives. You welcome a new neighbor because you'd want to be welcomed if you were the new neighbor. You have a fight with your sister and think of not going to her wedding, but you wouldn't want your sister not to come to your wedding, and so you go. This is basic moral navigation 101. Most of us turn to it whenever we wonder what's the right thing to do.

There's something just like the Golden Rule when it comes to making good decisions. I call it the Golden Law: Never do anything you wouldn't strongly advise your best friend to do in the same situation.

I have a really good dentist. I recently went to see him because I broke a tooth. My options were to get a crown or a "brilliant" (a compromise between a filling and a crown). After he ran through the pros and cons of each, he said, "Look, it's your decision, but if you were my brother I'd advise you to go for the crown." In other words, my dentist was advising me the way he would advise someone he cares about very much.

Why would we do anything less for ourselves? If you're in a troubled relationship and you're thinking of breaking up with your partner, you should ask yourself, "What would I advise my best friend?" You'd be amazed at how asking yourself that question could save you from destroying something wonderful just because you're going through a bad period.

You may wonder, "What does the way I'd advise others have to do with the kind of advice I give myself?" A lot. Talk to people who've made more than their share of bad decisions and you'll often hear them say, "If only I'd taken my own advice." Talk to people who've made a lot of good decisions and you'll often hear them say, "I did what I'd tell anyone else to do."

The Golden Law says we have what it takes to be great decision makers, just the way the Golden Rule says we have what it takes to be effective moral agents. The problem isn't that we don't have the right stuff. The problem is remembering to apply it.

"But I'm different"

People who make bad decisions can typically give just as good advice as people who make good decisions. The difference is that they don't take their own advice.

Let me tell you about Jeff, who owned a small shop in a trendy part of Cambridge selling the coolest, hippest, most interesting knickknacks and collectibles: metal advertising signs going back to the turn of the century. Old dolls. Wind-up toys from the fifties. Vinyl LPs with the campiest album covers you can imagine.

Sounds like a great market niche, but Jeff never made much of a living from his store. It took a lot of money and time to get the stock in, and it sold slowly. Things just couldn't keep going the same way. Jeff would have to start making new decisions.

Now his friend Mark shows up asking Jeff for advice. Mark is a locally renowned maker and designer of silver jewelry that uses a lot of semiprecious stones. Mark had been thinking of opening a retail outlet. "Look," Jeff said, "you need a cheap location that's near a good location. Everything else is marketing. You've got to get people to know about what you do, you've got to have buzz, you've got to have cachet. You've got to have trendy women wearing your stuff so that other women ask them where they bought it.

You've got to have your stuff carried at other select stores so that when people come directly to you they think they're getting the really good stuff for cheap . . ."

When Jeff went home the truth hit him: he was giving Mark advice he wasn't taking himself.

Why hadn't Jeff taken his own advice? He didn't see himself as a businessman who needed to worry about marketing. He was different.

This is one of the major excuses people use for why they don't take their own advice. They say:

- "My God, I'd kill my sister if she got involved with a guy like my boyfriend, Joey. But I'm different. I can take care of myself."

- "Guys know I work in the market and they come to me for investment advice. I always say put your money in a few good mutual funds and an index fund, and just leave it there. Of course I don't do that myself. I'm extremely active in day trading, options, and short selling. I know there are guys out there with their money in mutual funds who do better than I do, but I really think once I get the hang of all this there's a lot of money to be made."

The excuses go on and on. When players in the NBA talk to kids in school they tell them to practice a lot. The players who make good decisions follow this advice, even though with their talent you'd think they wouldn't need to. The players who make poor decisions exempt themselves from it and don't achieve what they're capable of.

If you give good advice, you're a good decision maker. If your record doesn't reflect your ability, start taking some of your own advice.

Taking your own advice

Let me introduce you to a whole new procedure for making big decisions. Pretend it's not you. Pretend it's people you care about instead.

Let's say there's a new job your friends are thinking of taking because it will boost their career. But they can't stand the idea of the initial pay cut they'd have to take and are tending toward declining that new job. What would you advise them? If you would tell them that this is an opportunity they can't pass up, and if they have to budget their finances for a while, so what—*that's your advice to you*. This is a great procedure for people trying to recover from an image of themselves as bad decision makers.

We're all better advice givers than we are decision makers. So give yourself the advice you'd give others. Making great decisions will then come easily.

Law #18

Appreciate the Newness
of Each Situation

Are you in danger of applying old learning to a new decision?

A RE you flexible or rigid? This is a very important question when it comes to decision making. The problem is that people who are rigid don't think of themselves that way. They're proud of having firm convictions. They congratulate themselves on the lessons they've learned. And that's fine, except for one thing. Rigid people approach new situations as if they were just like previous situations. They are not free to appreciate the way a new opportunity may differ from similar-seeming ones in the past.

Decision making is the way you and I express our freedom. But if you and I aren't free to see how a new situation is different from situations in the past, the freedom to choose is an illusion.

A fresh-eyed heroine

My mother-in-law, Sonia, is a woman of great strength and intelligence. She grew up in Poland, the daughter of a poor Jewish farmer. When the Nazis came in 1939, she fled east to Uzbekistan, in Central Asia. As the years of exile lengthened, she found a way to make a living while raising a son and then a daughter, my future wife.

After the war, Sonia faced an enormous decision about where

to go. Uzbekistan was where she'd been safe, but Communism was too oppressive. Poland was destroyed, and she assumed that her parents and probably all of her nine brothers and sisters had been killed. She thought of America or Israel, but she didn't know how to get to either place.

But if she didn't know how to get to America, she knew how to get to *Americans*—they were in Germany, where they had created military bases and camps for displaced persons. Many people told her she was crazy. Germany was where the Nazis had been, they said; why go to the land of the Nazis? The thing to do is to stay as far away from there as possible.

The last thing in the world Sonia wanted was to go to Germany, but going there was the only way to get to Americans and, eventually, to America. With her baby and four-year-old in tow, she traveled on foot and in horse-pulled carts through Central Asia and Communist East Europe.

She and her children even hid under a pile of hay at a Communist checkpoint. If one of the kids had cried, everyone would've been killed. They made it through to Germany and to the American soldiers.

As a decision maker, Sonia had the gift of flexibility. She was able to see that Germany, which had been a place of danger, was now a place of safety. She used her inner freedom to create a new life.

That's what this law is all about. To be one of those people who make good decisions, you must be able to appreciate the uniqueness of each situation. You're considering an option today that's seemingly similar to an option you faced once before. In the meantime you've learned lessons. And you're proud of what you've learned. Here's the problem: are you so proud of what you've learned that you'll be unable to see how the new option is in fact different from the old one?

That's why learning can be dangerous. Learning teaches you to respond to the new by using what you've discovered about the old. That's good if the new is like the old. It's bad if the new is nothing like the old.

It's all too easy to apply lessons from one situation to another that may or may not be similar. My mother-in-law understood that applying the lesson "Germany Is Bad for Jews" made sense during the Nazi era but didn't make sense afterward, particularly if you were trying to get out of Europe.

When we don't see how things have changed

Interestingly, my mother was a very good businesswoman like my mother-in-law. She was cofounder of a major chain of dance studios and an excellent saleswoman. She must have had an intuitive appreciation of this law, because you can't sell to people without being able to zero in on an individual's unique buying motive.

But there was one way my mother got hurt by failing to use this law. As a child of the Depression, she saw Wall Street as a place of danger and loss. Like millions of other Americans she was terrified that what had happened once could happen again. In postwar America, when others were slowly growing fortunes in the stock market, my mother's fear of another crash made her keep her money in a bank savings account where inflation ate it up.

My mother didn't learn when *not* to learn from the past. She was proud of "having learned her lesson." But in fact this prevented her from adapting to a new situation that would've brought her more choices and greater freedom.

Becoming free and open

Of course you should be proud of the lessons you've learned in life. But you should be just as proud of your ability to see how a new situation is different and how the old lessons sometimes don't apply.

Here's an example. Each time we begin a new relationship, how many of us focus primarily on avoiding the disaster that led to the end of the previous relationship? The last woman you were involved with, for instance, was bright but difficult. The next woman you start seeing is bright too, so you think you'd better stay away from her—she'll probably be difficult. So you start looking for a woman who's sweet but dumb. But how can you tell who's really sweet? You can tell very quickly who's dumb. So you find someone dumb who seems sweet, and you spend a few years discovering how being involved with someone who's not your intellectual equal can drag you down.

People who bounce from one unsatisfactory relationship to another tend to overapply the lesson from the past situation. I know a guy who's an admiral. A long time ago he fell in love with a beauty queen who ended up cheating on him. So he "learned a lesson." He said to himself, "Beautiful women will cheat on you. Marry someone plain and you'll be safe." That's what he did, and it was a disaster because he was not attracted to his wife.

He'd thought he was making a good decision because he was avoiding the previous disaster. But he would've done better if he'd learned *nothing* from his disaster with the beauty queen. There are a lot of different ways people can hurt us. Drawing oversimplified "lessons" the way he'd done was a big mistake.

How much better off my friend the admiral would have been if he'd found someone attractive, who was a good person and shared his interests—the basic things we all look for in a partner. That way he could have treated each new relationship as a new situation to be evaluated on its own terms. As an admiral he should have known: don't fight the last war.

In each area of their lives, people who make great decisions are careful not to apply mechanically lessons from the past that don't apply in the present.

Always ask yourself: "What's special and different about this new situation?" The answers you come up with will make it possible for you to deal with this new situation on its own terms.

Law #19

Make Yourself Proud

Which decision will give you self-respect?

M OST of us take for granted that we'll do whatever's necessary to maintain our self-respect. We certainly avoid doing
anything we know would kick dents in our self-respect.

It sounds basic and obvious, doesn't it? That's the problem. It's
too basic, and too obvious. Yes, we care about self-respect, but too
often when it comes to making a big decision, we make the mis-
ake of taking our self-respect for granted. And that's where we can
get into trouble. We assume our self-respect will just be there no
matter what we do, no matter how badly we neglect it. Because if
you're not nourishing your self-respect, you're neglecting it.

People who make great choices never forget that self-respect
plays an important role in their figuring out what to do.

---

*When faced with two options, all else being equal, good decision
makers choose the one that will make themselves the most
proud. When they don't know what to do, they search for options
by asking, "What will make me proud?"*

Losing self-respect
Let's not kid ourselves that it's always easy. Look at Amy. Like a lot of
idealistic young people, she became a lawyer to make the world a better place. A born litigator, Amy figured she'd help the downtrodden

fight for what was theirs. But idealism is constantly threatened by materialism. As she approached graduation and the job offers trickled in, Amy quickly saw that the money and prestige and excitement that were up for grabs had nothing to do with the downtrodden.

Amy took a well-paying job with a firm that represented corporations. She figured that it would be good experience she could use in the future to help the downtrodden.

Five years later Amy was still there, on track to making partner. But she was bored and her life felt empty.

Then Amy met Arthur, a wealthy venture capitalist who made her head spin with visions of changing the world with new businesses. It all seemed very exciting and important.

They fell in love, got married, and discussed having children. Soon Amy was faced with a decision of whether to become a stay-at-home mom. Arthur's work was important, unlike her own. The decision was easy for her.

Ten years later, Amy felt like an exhibit in the Museum of Devolution. Arthur was a success but she felt like a failure. Instead of participating in courtroom dramas, she was mediating domestic dramas over sharing toys. Amy knew that theoretically what she was doing was noble and valuable. But it didn't feel that way. Instead of helping the downtrodden, she was feeling downtrodden herself.

You don't have to be a lawyer to understand, and empathize with, the pattern of choices Amy made that ended up attacking her self-respect. These choices could easily have been avoided. Way back when Amy was looking over her job offers she simply forgot to ask herself, "What about my self-respect? What will happen to me if I go in this new direction I'm thinking of going and abandon my dreams of helping the downtrodden?"

By practicing a form of law she didn't respect Amy hurt herself. When self-respect gets undermined, it leads to problems. For Amy it led to her being unable to stick with her values.

Taking care of your self-respect

People who make great decisions take care of their self-respect. How do you do this? First of all, always *focus on the most important thing.* If you can't identify it, ask: which option will make me most proud in the long run?

The right way to gain self-respect

When you sense you're falling behind, it's tempting to boost your self-respect by telling people what you're going to do. The guy who says he's going to start day trading so he can become a multi-millionaire will impress some people at the beginning, but reserve judgment until you see his track record a year later.

This is serious business. It's not about what you launch; it's about where it will take you.

Finding the right approach when it comes to maintaining self-respect requires two things:

1. You have to know what gives *you* self-respect. Everyone is different. Some people, for example, need to make money. If they help the downtrodden but don't make money, no abstract morality will make them feel good about themselves. It all depends on how you work as an individual.

2. You have to be realistic about what will happen to your self-respect as your decision plays out. Many situations that have the potential to damage your self-respect involve illusions of necessity. You think you can't leave your job out of necessity even though your boss is demeaning. Necessity is real, but self-respect is a necessity too.

If you're looking at options, ask what each will do to your self-respect. Then pick the one that does the most for it. The answer might not be obvious, but winners at least look for the answer.

Law #20

Pay Attention to the Big, Fat, Obvious Issues

What are you overlooking?

Few things have impressed me more in my research than the value of this simple law. When we're trying to make a decision, we try to be "smart." For too many of us, being "smart" means looking for the subtle and the complex. We're embarrassed to go with the obvious.

Great decision makers don't worry about being "smart." They understand that the big, fat, obvious issues in any decision are in fact enormously important, and they give them full weight. When you take a look at people who made wonderful decisions, you'll hear them say over and over, "Well, it was so obvious . . ."

Finding what's obvious

Your sister's Doberman just had puppies and she's insisting that you take one. You live alone in a small apartment in the city and you work. Do you give in to your sister?

Hello! A temporarily miffed sister versus a soon-to-be-psychotic Doberman locked in your apartment every day? It's just *obvious* what your choice should be.

Your sister is a distraction. The cuteness of the puppy is a distraction. The big thing—big as a dead moose in the middle of a narrow country road—is *Hello!* it's a Doberman. There are always confusing, distracting issues that clamor for your attention. But you simply don't let them force you to neglect the obvious.

Eisenhower invaded France with all of the Allied troops. But where to land? There were a hundred and one things to consider. Ike went with the obvious. He found the beachhead with the fewest German troops, gaining surprise by giving the enemy no indication about where and when he was landing. Others agonized. Eisenhower saw what was obvious and won.

Lead us not into temptation

So you see how to apply this law. You ask yourself what's the obvious factor to consider, and you go with that.

We have to overcome psychological potholes that make us ignore the obvious. Avoid these potholes and you'll be fine.

Psychological pothole #1: Giving equal weight to unequal factors

Never let lesser considerations outweigh more important considerations. A guy I know was wondering whether to marry a certain woman. She was beautiful, smart, loving, and wonderfully sane, but she wasn't interested in joining him in intellectual conversations, something he enjoyed. He almost lost her. He was saved when he realized that intellectually stimulating after-dinner chitchat wasn't close to being as important to him as finding someone beautiful, smart, loving, and wonderfully sane.

When an option scores high in all the big, important areas, you don't walk away from it because of a small imperfection unless you're a character on *Seinfeld*. Not when it's really hard to find a partner as terrific as the woman he'd found.

Psychological pothole #2: Wanting to show how clever you are

The obvious is *obvious*. You don't win genius points for seeing it. People who want to seem clever often make a point of ignoring the obvious. That's why wise guys make poor decisions.

Take the world of investment. It's tough to make a buck, and there are no shortcuts. The obvious thing here is that the best investors who work at it full-time and are paid millions rarely beat the market averages by more than a couple of points, year in and year out. Furthermore, someone who had a special secret that would allow him to do better than this would never, ever sell it because he could never make as much money selling his secret as he could using his secret.

And yet every day there are people who think they are so clever that the obvious doesn't apply to them. And they all get creamed. Just look at what happens long-term to day traders, speculators in options and penny stocks, people who pursue hot tips, to say nothing of the masterminds behind the collapse of ventures like Long-Term Capital Management.

You can be too smart: it begins the moment your cleverness makes you ignore the obvious.

Psychological pothole #3: Your hope gets in the way

Hope is a good thing, except when it, like cleverness, prevents you from seeing the obvious. Suppose you're starting to get involved with someone who's an alcoholic just like your father, who walked out on your mother. Who knows why you hope this guy will be different? But you're in danger if your hope blinds you to the obvious, that this guy's a loser and if he were literally the last man in the world you'd still need to stay away from him.

There's always hope for everyone. People can and do change, in amazing ways. But it's just as obvious that you don't hitch your future to someone with big problems.

Psychological pothole #4: Your negativity gets in the way

A lawyer I know gained a reputation for the excellent work she did specializing in computer software litigation. It was a growing area to which few brought an MIT degree in software engineering, as she had. Unfortunately, she was stuck at a mediocre law firm where she'd have trouble pursuing the legal issues that interested her. Everyone told her that she should go off on her own—whatever she invested would be repaid within a year. But she was scared to leave because she was in line for a partnership.

Her negativity dragged her down. She had endless worries.

Each was partly reasonable, yet the obvious thing was that no one was doing what she was doing at that time and that the only way to unlock her true value would be to go off on her own.

Unfortunately, she waited too long. She made partner, but her energies were wasted; eventually other people moved into her area and focused on what she could have focused on. She got trumped even though she'd held all the cards.

Look at your alternatives. Look at the considerations you're weighing. Then ask yourself what's obvious and go with it. That way you'll become one of those great decision makers who can respond to compliments by saying, "Well, it was really obvious . . ."

Law #21

Never Forget Why You Made Your Decision

Are you judging yourself with different criteria from what you first used?

$\mathbf{P}$ART of making good choices is *feeling* good about the choices you make. You'll never feel good about your choices if you use different criteria for judging your choices from what you used for making them.

Let's say you're going to plant a fruit tree in your backyard. You decide you want apples, but all the best apple trees take several years before they produce good fruit, or even any fruit at all. But there's this one variety of tree that you're told will produce apples faster than the others. They'll be smaller and less sweet, but you're impatient and you tell yourself it'll be nice just to have the apples.

Two years later the apples come, and indeed they are quite small and tart.

Did you make a good decision?

People who typically make good decisions say, "I knew what I wanted, I knew what I was giving up to get it, I got what I wanted, and I'm happy."

People who make bad decisions say, "I wanted fruit fast and I got it, but this fruit is so disappointing I regret the whole thing." They're either stuck with something they don't like or they now have to do what they should have done in the first place—get the apple tree that grows slowly—although they've wasted time along the way.

Switching games

People who make great decisions never make a decision based on one set of criteria and then later judge themselves using a different set of criteria.

Changing your criteria is called *switching games*. You do it when you play one game (the fast fruit game, for example) and then judge yourself by the rules of another game (the great fruit game). And it's a tragedy. There you are, winning the game you set out to play, and you feel like a loser because you suddenly judge yourself by a completely different set of rules. Talk about snatching defeat from the jaws of victory!

Kim's story

Kim arrived in Boston fifteen years ago to attend the Berklee College of Music, an incubator of countless well-known rock, pop, and jazz musicians. But Kim thought that the whole music scene, especially rock, was too much about money. Kim wanted a career in anticommercial, alternative rock.

"You know, it's going to be tough to make a living from that," her bass guitar teacher said.

Kim knew. But the path Kim was choosing was not necessarily a bad decision. It might have been a great decision for her, as long as it was based on her truly knowing herself, knowing what she needed, knowing what she was getting into, knowing what her priorities were, and most of all knowing what was most important to her.

She knew there'd be years, maybe a whole life, of day jobs— working in record stores, waitressing, maybe some teaching. So what? Kim was walking into her future with her eyes open.

Imagine pages flying off calendars, like shots in old movies that show the passage of time. Today Kim is a known alternative rocker, with a great reputation, although she hates the word "alternative." "Hey, I'm just a rock chick. I just do my own thing." She's heading up her third group, which gets a few gigs, but not many, and they don't pay much.

Kim is also raising her ten-year-old daughter, Ananda. The prospect of a bleak financial future and seeing people she went to school with make more money in the last week than she made all last year, really started to get to her.

Now was Kim's decision a good or bad decision?

That depends on which game she's playing—the "starving alternative rock artist" game? The "making it in commercial music" game? Or the "I want a safe career" game?

Kim started switching games with a vengeance. Earlier she'd played the alternative rocker game and won it, making her decision a good one. Later she started feeling like a failure because she was judging herself by the rules of the other two games.

She'd planted the tree of her dreams, and when it started to bear exactly the fruit she'd expected, she wanted to chop it down.

It's too bad. Kim is deprived of feeling that her decision was perfect for her, according to everything she knows about herself, everything she used to value, everything she still values. The things she misses—money, worldly success, security—are still lower priorities even now. It's true that Kim is seeing what she's missed out on. Yet she knows she wouldn't have decided differently if she could go back and do it all over again. So why should she suffer regret just because she's aware of the price she paid?

Regret prevention

As you think about how some decision of yours will play out over time, *ask yourself what will happen to your priorities.*

If before you make your decision you think there's a good chance your priorities will shift, then be careful. You're at risk of making a choice that later on will feel very bad to you. It will certainly be a choice that will make you feel you've wasted your time.

Here's what I recommend to everyone making a decision for which there's even the slightest risk of regret. Write a letter to yourself about what you're choosing and why. Make your priorities clear.

For example, you might say, "I'm going to Wall Street to spend my life making money. My priorities are making money and being in the game of making money. If I make a lot of money, I'll feel I've won." Now picture yourself as a driven, Maalox-chugging Wall Street tycoon. Read that letter you wrote to yourself again. Will you think of your earlier self as a blind, ridiculous fool for having those priorities?

In other words, can you look your future self in the eye, with those priorities of yours, whatever they are, and still feel good about yourself? After all, a decision is a kind of deal you're making with your future self, because it's your future self who will be judging the outcome. You're foolish if you don't bring your future self into the decision-making process and get his or her approval.

Kim could've done this. She certainly believed in what she was doing. She was warranted in this belief. Her future self, whom we've actually met, held the same priorities.

Fortunately Kim made peace with the life she'd chosen. She accepted the fact that the price she paid was bigger than she'd thought it would be. But the price of not staying true to her musical dream would have been even bigger.

Insuring yourself

Kim made the mistake of not doing what I call *buying priority-shift insurance*. You do this when you hold fast to your priorities but buy protection for highly predictable ways your priorities might change.

Kim could easily have said, "I'm an alternative rocker. It's just that I know that as you get older money, accomplishment, and security mean more. So let me start putting money away for myself now. It's not all or nothing."

It's not all or nothing. That is the understanding people who make good decisions bring to situations in which their priorities might shift. They take care of their priorities today and they spend a little time and energy insuring for shifting priorities tomorrow.

You never have to feel regret. If your choices fit you and your priorities, regret will rarely be an issue anyway. If you're aware that your priorities might change and you buy yourself a little insurance and take care of some of those future priorities, then there will be even less potential for regret.

Whenever you make a decision, know why you're making it, know your values and beliefs, and then use those same values and beliefs to judge the outcomes of your decision. Congratulate yourself on making a good decision if you got the outcome you should have expected in the beginning.

Knowing When You've Made a Great Choice

H ow do you know when you've made a great choice?
You'd think it would be easy, but in life, sometimes, results can seem murky. Sometimes things turn out great but the cost
is high. Sometimes things don't turn out as you'd hoped, but
maybe that's still for the best. Sometimes it takes quite a while before you actually know how things have turned out. Was Ronald
Reagan's decision to run for president a good decision for him?
After all, he failed the first two times. You can't always judge by in-
stant success. If we did, we'd all be in trouble.

So, how do people know they've made a good decision? Let's
ask the experts, people who consistently, time after time, make
more than their share of good decisions. How do they evaluate
their decisions?

First, they feel good about the way they made the decision
If you can't control outcomes, at least you can control processes. If
you cautiously make a decision, focus on what's most important to
you, and base your decision on what you want and who you are,
how can you not feel good about that?

Take two very different decisions: where to go to college and
whether to have another child. Both can be really tough, highly
emotionally charged decisions. With both there can be no way of

knowing ultimately whether you did the best thing. But research that looks into the connections among autonomy, self-efficacy, and overall happiness makes clear that people who listened to themselves, based their decision on what they cared about, and felt they had time to make the decision also felt good about the decision itself.

Process matters.

Second, they feel better about the decision as time goes by

You may not necessarily feel wildly ecstatic about your decision the moment you make it. Doubts may linger. Events may transpire that threaten the outcome you were hoping for. Yet as time passes, you feel better about your decision, in these ways:

- You're proud of your decision and proud of yourself for making it.

- You have no regrets. There's little looking back at what might have been and what you could have done.

- You feel an increasing sense of commitment. Many people make the mistake of thinking they have to feel committed before they decide. That's not how great decision makers operate. They understand that if you have to wait for total commitment before you decide, either you're a fool or you'll never be able to act. Commitment is not a gift you bring to your decision. *Commitment is a gift a good decision brings to you after you've made it.*

- You have the feeling that you're coming home to yourself. We all know what home means: a place of safety and comfort; a place set up by you and for you. Your decision should make you feel at home.

- Your decision makes you happy. This may not happen right away, but why else do we make decisions if not to make ourselves happy?

- You feel free. Good decisions give us the sense that we've opened doors for ourselves. You have more of the kinds of choices you want.

Now you know what to look for. Just follow Dr. Foster's thirty laws and you will find it.

Law #22

Know What's Real

What realities will affect your decision?

I N the card game of life, reality trumps everything. Great decision makers know how to be hopeful while at the same time
keeping a clear-eyed sense of reality. Not taking reality into account has far bigger costs than merely making bad decisions. When
you ignore reality, you get your brains beat in. When that happens
more than a couple of times, you can get really discouraged.

Ask anyone who's tried to climb Mt. Everest. The mountain is
reality. Understand and respect that reality, and you'll have a
chance. Ignore that reality and you'll end up in big, big trouble.

But why would any of us ignore reality? We're smart, and we
have some experience of the world. What gets us in trouble is
hope and desire. We pin our hopes on some outcome. There's
something we desire with all our hearts. And that prevents us from
seeing what's real. Don't misunderstand me. Hope and desire are
wonderful. Just not when they blind you to reality.

I think about what one father did when he saw that his son was
an underachiever in school, unmotivated and uninterested in
studying and getting good grades. The father himself had been that
way, and he'd suffered for it. He was now a huge success as a management consultant, but there'd been years of struggle, years in
which he wasn't taken seriously because he'd graduated from a
third-rate college.

The father "knew" that his kid was bright. This gave him hope that his kid could do better. He certainly had all the desire in the world for his kid to do better. So he decided to go on the warpath and make an all-out frontal assault starting with his son's sophomore year in high school. Using powerful punishments and rewards, he would make his son become motivated. He did this in spite of the fact that he'd talked to a well-respected educational psychologist who told him that you can't force-feed motivation, that kids either have it or they don't.

But the father didn't want to see what was real. Sure the kid wanted to please his father, but studying was unpleasant. The more the father pushed, the more the son thought his father hated him. He started losing interest in wanting to please a father who refused to see him and love him as he really was—a good kid who just wasn't into studying.

The kid graduated from high school with a C+ average; his relationship with his father was so damaged that years and years were needed for any healing to occur. And none of this pain and waste would have happened if the father had seen what was real.

Seeing what's real is something we're all capable of and is a vital ingredient in every good decision. If we can untangle the forces that prevent us from respecting reality, we can be freed forever from the danger of violating this law.

As you face a decision you're going to be fueled by hope and desire. But if you want to save yourself from making a bad decision, ask yourself the question that people who make great decisions ask themselves: "How does what I want to be true prevent me from checking out what really is true?"

Still, seeing what's really real can be hard. So I asked people who were great decision makers what laws of reality they felt were most powerful, most common, and most deserving of respect. Using their responses, I came up with the following list:

The Top Ten Realities

1. *You always have to give a lot.* Whatever you get into—from business to sports to marriage, the realistic expectation is that you're probably going to put in a lot more than it feels like you're getting back.

2. *Money's always a bigger deal than you think it will be.* You'll always need more money. Everything takes more money than you'd predict.

3. *You'll always need more time.* However long you think it will take to do something, count on its actually taking longer. And everything you do that's new to you will take far, far longer than you can possibly imagine.

4. *You're never as important to other people as they are to you.* If you need other people to come through for you, expect that they'll be busy, distracted, and generally putting less emphasis on what you care about than you do.

5. *Expect surprises, good and bad.* Wildly unpredictable outcomes are the one thing you can always predict. On those rare occasions when everything works out as planned, it's because you paid others a lot of money to make it work.

6. *Things always get more complicated over time.* Whenever you think of how your options will play out—an event, a relationship, whatever—assume that simplicity will always be the first casualty.

7. *There are more ways things can go wrong than go right.* Problems appear. Obstacles and roadblocks crop up. Disappointments happen.

8. *Most victorious enterprises are put together with bubble gum and spit.* In the real world you can't nail everything down before you launch a decision. Good decision makers adjust their jerry-built fixes as they go along.

9. *You're going to need a lot of help.* Like the Pyramids, like the Great Wall of China, every great decision is built with the

assistance and participation of a lot of people. You need to bring on board everyone who might be impacted by your decision.

10. *Don't pretend to be different from who you really are, and don't try to deny what you really want.* Of all the realities, you yourself are the reality you have to respect the most.

Do things always work out exactly the way these reality statements say they will? Of course not. Sometimes you get lucky. But if you want to bet on how things will turn out, this is where the smart money places its bets.

Holding on to reality

Most of us know these realities. So why do many of us forget them? If we can answer that question, we'll have everything we need to avoid being ambushed again. Here are the four major reasons people blind themselves to realities that should be easy to see.

They don't check out their assumptions
Most people don't get into trouble because they literally ignore what's real. They get into trouble because they think they know what's real *but they are wrong.*

Take Jim, my favorite real estate gazillionaire. He has the utter confidence that comes from knowing he's made a lot of great decisions.

But no one is invulnerable. Look at the decision facing Jim now. He's married to a woman he hasn't loved in a long time. He's fallen in love with a woman he's not married to.

Jim has to decide which woman he wants to be with. The key question in Jim's mind is whether this other woman is really as great as she seems. Is she a diamond or a shard of glass?

"How do you know she's not just interested in you for your money?" Jim's best friend asked him.

Listen to Jim's overconfidence. "I know it's not about my money," Jim said, "because she just isn't a person who makes money the center of her life. So I believe her when she says that nice as the money is it has absolutely nothing to do with whether she wants to be with me or not. She even offered to sign a pre-nup!"

You may have heard that when someone says it's not about the money, it's about the money. With Jim's lady friend, it really was about the money. In fact, she hadn't been interested in him until a major deal elevated him into the big leagues. That's when she started pushing him to leave his wife. That's when she seemed to be interested only in the things Jim was interested in. Everyone saw this but Jim. And in fact her loud offer to sign the pre-nup was accompanied by endless delaying and evasive tactics. They eventually got married (sans pre-nup) and she took him to the cleaners.

Jim screwed up because he fell victim to one of the most common reasons people fail to respect reality:

The consequences of seeing what's real are too frightening or painful. If you see what's real, you're going to have to act on it, and you don't want to because it's too much trouble. Blindness is simply easier and less scary than facing reality.

To seriously check out his lady friend Jim would've had to face the possibility of losing her, maybe because he wouldn't have liked what he found, maybe because she would've gotten upset and left. Where would Jim have been then? No wonderful, sexy, affectionate lady friend. No hope of happiness. Just being stuck with a boring wife he hated.

Every time you're convinced you know what's real, *check it out anyway*. Fairy tales don't usually come true. Be careful: the smarter and shrewder and more sophisticated you are, the more likely you are to mistake a fairy tale for reality. Not because you're a boob, but because your self-confidence will do you in.

They fall victim to flattery

This is the second most common reason people fail to respect reality:

The story you're presented with is so flattering, or the situation you're facing is so seductive, that you're almost literally mesmerized into forgetting to check out reality.

It's simply the case that Jim had never been treated so nicely by a woman. This woman dangled the prospect of paradise in front of Jim. But it was a very special paradise. It was built out of flattery. Here's a deep secret: Most people don't feel so great about themselves. Even cocksure, arrogant, swaggering models and moguls. No drug is more intoxicating and addictive than flattery. No drug is more likely to blind you to what's real.

If you're facing a decision and one of your options flatters and seduces you, check it out. There are job offers that are flattering. It can be very flattering if some big shot you know offers you a stock tip. But the more you're flattered, the more you need to check it out.

They get carried away by their hobby horses

Jenny got fired last week, unceremoniously thrown out on her ass, and this in the tony world of Boston money management. What could she have done to earn that?

Thousands of Dow points ago, Jenny, who was paid to actively manage the trust funds of some very rich people, made a big bad decision: to give the advice that owning stocks was bad; they were too expensive.

She arranged her clients' portfolios so that they would have very little exposure to stocks. Cash and bonds were good. Natural resources were good. No stocks.

For three years, while everyone else was making money, Jenny's clients went nowhere. And yet Jenny didn't change. She didn't see what millions of people were able to see and appreciate, a story of liquidity and new paradigms. Jenny's main allegiance wasn't to the truth of the world, it was to her little hobby horse, that stocks were priced too high.

And that leads us to the third most common reason people fail to respect reality:

They have some pet theory, and they act as if they're much more interested in assuming it's true than in letting reality test its validity.

All Jenny needed to do was admit she was wrong, but that can be incredibly hard. She'd have to give up the view that she possessed special insight into the market. She'd have to admit she wasted years in poor investment strategies for her clients.

How do you abandon your hobby horse? Get a new hobby horse. I have a tip: the best hobby horse of all is a passion to ferret out real change. Goodness knows it's not easy, but if your beliefs don't catch up to the ways the world is changing, you and your hobby horse will get left behind.

They get lazy

If you're facing a decision, you have hunches about reality that point you toward one option or another. To save yourself from disaster, you must check out whether your beliefs are preventing you from seeing reality. If you don't do this work, you're lazy and disaster will follow.

For example, you want to get into advertising and you're offered a job in the accounting department of an ad agency. You're told people are promoted out of the accounting department all the time to become creative ad makers. You'd like this to be true, but is it?

The enemy is laziness. That's the fourth most common reason people fail to respect reality:

In some ways it's easier to slide toward disaster than to see what's real. It takes work to examine your assumptions, it takes legwork to get the facts, and it's arduous to reconstruct your life when you discover some pet belief is false.

Here's something you hear great decision makers say all the time: "Well, let me just check out whether this is true or not."

How would you do that at the ad agency? You have to talk to people. You have to find the names of people to talk to. You have to get them on the phone. You might have to call them back a number of times. All this is hard if you're lazy.

But nothing is harder than having to cope with the results of a bad decision.

We don't like to see what's real because it feels like cold water poured over a cherished dream. But that's the wrong way to think of it. If it really is a jungle out there, seeing what's real is the only protection you've got. It's an early warning system of danger. It's a compass to show you your way.

Law #23

Get What You Need to Make Your Decision a Success

Are you equipped to carry out this decision?

I HAVE good news for you. The only reason a lot of decisions go bad is that one critical piece of equipment, one strategic resource, was missing. If you'd had it, your decision would have worked out great. The only difference between bread that rises and bread that fails to rise is yeast. Do you know what the yeast is in your next decision?

People get in trouble when they leave out a key ingredient. For example, you and your buddy were going to drive cross-country to see America. It had sounded like such a great idea. Your car was old but you thought, so what? Here's what: In the middle of nowhere your car died, and you didn't have the money to fix it. You were stuck in a terrible jam. No car, no dough.

Lots of decisions bring us to a place like this. A decision isn't just about going on a road trip. It's about knowing what you need to make the trip successful and enjoyable. Carrying through the decision from the beginning, to the middle, and on to the end. It's the whole journey, not the first day of the journey. This law is designed for you to ask: *How do I carry out my decision to completion?*

When you decide to do something—whether you're traveling cross-country, buying a dog, starting a business, or getting married—you're deciding to do all the things that come with carrying

out that decision successfully. Most of us are well equipped to do
this.

**People who make good decisions remember to ask themselves
what they'll need to carry out their decision successfully, and
they don't accept glib answers.**

Here are the four most important forms of resources, support,
and help that people need to carry out most decisions successfully:

Money
As you and your buddy found out on the road, you need to have
enough money to carry your decision to completion. People who
make great decisions follow two simple guidelines when it comes
to thinking ahead about money.

- You always have to think about how much money you'll need

- You always need more money than you think you'll need

Let's now say you want to buy a house in a nice neighborhood
in a major metropolitan area. With typical mortgage payments,
property taxes, and insurance, your annual housing expenses could
easily be fifty thousand dollars. That's money going out before
you've even put a nickel's worth of food in your mouth.

Most people who've recently bought a house have discovered
this: There's a huge gap between what you think you can afford
and what you can afford. When you add up all the hidden expenses, you find you can't afford the house that at first glance you
thought you could just barely manage.

People who make great decisions understand that they always
need more money than they think they will.

So if you're buying a house, for example, how do you set up realistic expectations? First scale back to the most realistic expectations you can imagine. Then scale back even further, because as
expensive as things seem even when you've cut down to the min-

imum, you have still left out major expenditures that you can't begin to fathom even now. For example, people who buy a new house almost always spend more on furniture and furnishings than they thought they would.

People who make more than their share of bad choices will do a slapdash job of thinking about how much money they'll need. And before they know it, they're in a lot of trouble.

This is a huge issue when it comes to starting your own business. Part of being very careful when it comes to thinking about money is being very careful thinking about how fast money will roll in.

Take Sammy. "I talked to people," he said, "and everyone said they'd be happy to drive half an hour to get to a restaurant that really knew how to cook steak. Well, you draw a half-hour-driving-time circle around this location I've scouted, and you've got a huge pool of potential customers for Sammy's Steak-n-Stuff."

I spoke to Sammy recently, and he was surprised at the low turnout. "How long does it take for people to find out about a good steak place and recommend it to their friends and start making repeat visits?" he asked.

Sammy should have checked out his assumptions by talking to other restaurant owners. They would have told him about the difference between potential and actual customers and how long it can take to turn a potential into an actual customer. Then and only then would Sammy have been able to make a good guess about whether he could build up a customer base before his money ran out.

The point is that you need to do a good job of thinking about how much money you'll need to make any decision of yours a success, and "good job" usually means being extremely cautious about saying what "enough money" is.

Advice

Most decisions you make will take you to an unfamiliar place. There will be new challenges, and questions you never imagined asking. Who will be there to give you good advice?

Getting good advice is like getting good directions when you're lost. How else do you find your way?

If someone tells me about a business they're starting, I can almost always predict how successful they'll be just by asking, "Who are the advisers you've brought on board?" A well-respected local CPA? A person successful in a similar business? Someone who represents important suppliers or customers? If there are people like this on board as advisers, success is far likelier than if the advisers are the usual random assortment of inexperienced acquaintances and relatives.

Believe it or not, this issue has powerful implications throughout our country. Consider kids growing up in disadvantaged surroundings. Who makes it and who doesn't? The data on resiliency is dramatic: people who climb out of the depths have one person they can point to—an older sibling, a grandmother, an uncle, a teacher, a neighbor—who believed in them enough to give advice and showed they cared enough to help the child along.

When it comes to your decisions, not having good advisers will almost certainly doom even those decisions that look great on paper. At the same time, great advisers can make a success out of a mediocre decision.

Yes, I know how easy it is to rationalize going forward without having good advisers in place. The rationales are all versions of "I don't need them"/ "I can't find them." These are very seductive. But you do need them. And you'd better find them. If you don't, you'll get creamed.

Time

You can always count on two things to take more time than you imagined. One is searching. The other is obtaining success.

This is good; now you know a simple truth that's easy to act on. Does one of the options you're considering involve searching? Or does it involve trying to become successful? Then you have entered the sticky time zone where everything takes a long time. Make sure you give yourself enough time for your decision to work itself out.

One of the places where people constantly make mistakes is in the search for love. They don't understand that finding the right person takes time. They inevitably waste time dating clearly inappropriate people and then, exhausted and disappointed, they waste time taking long breaks from dating.

The next thing they know ten or more years have gone and they still haven't found the right person. And if they don't change their patterns they could use up another ten years.

Good decision makers will counsel you to put time on your side: First, never waste time with losers. Second, never stop prospecting for possibilities. Third, know yourself, because that's the only way to know who will really fit you. People who do this find they've bought the only insurance you can against running out of time for real love.

Hope and commitment

A Wall Street trader who'd made more money by age forty than he knew what to do with, decided to move to Tennessee and become a fish farmer. But Nashville was not Manhattan, and fish farming was even harder than making money on Wall Street. So what? Here's what. This New Yorker was a fish out of water down there in Nashville. He felt he had no one to talk to. When fish farming turned into tough, discouraging work, how could this guy hold on to his hope and commitment when he had no support system?

Hope is precious and we need to protect it. When hope is eroded, we lose our ability to fix bad decisions or work at carrying out good ones.

We all need different things to maintain hope. The transplanted fish farmer needed people to talk to. You have to figure out what you need to keep you going should you get discouraged.

Money, advice, time, and hope are the big resources we all need as we carry forward our decisions. Don't turn an otherwise good decision into a bad decision because you've failed to have enough resources when you start.

Law #24

Find and Follow an Expert

Are you making sure you're relying on smart advisers?

Two of the greatest French monarchs, a thousand years apart, were Charlemagne and Napoleon. Both created empires and became emperors. Both led huge armies. One died full of years, full of honors, at the peak of his power, able to hand on everything he'd accomplished to his successors. The other died a failure, in disgrace, with everything he'd accomplished in ruins. One surrounded himself with wise advisers to whom he listened carefully. The other listened to no one.

Charlemagne was a proven fighter and general who made good decisions every step of the way. He never committed himself to campaigns he couldn't win, and even his endless battles against the Saxons were productive. Throughout his reign Charlemagne surrounded himself with the wisest men in his kingdom and listened carefully to what they had to say.

Napoleon overextended himself, alienated everyone, brought the wrath of the world down upon him, and did irreparable harm to the country he was supposed to protect. And no one could talk to him.

Does this law apply to those of us who aren't emperors? Yes! You're never such a big shot that you outgrow your need to consult experts. People who make bad decisions rely only on themselves, or else they consult only those who have no real expertise.

Just because someone's available to give advice doesn't mean he has good advice to give.

People who make great decisions work hard and make actual sacrifices to discover true experts in whatever area they're needing to make a decision. They have a deep humility that tells them to seek out advisers who are smarter and more experienced.

For example, I've been a consultant to a woman who's a well-respected judge. She's single and trying to decide whether to have children on her own. There are dangers and difficulties on every side of this decision. But as long as she's talking to smart, experienced people (and I'm not the only expert she's talking to), we can be confident that she will make a good decision, one that's right for her.

Looking beyond your friends

What about your friends? They're the advisers most of us turn to first. But are they your best advisers?

With every big decision you need a qualified adviser, someone who's unbiased, who has wide-ranging life experience, and who genuinely has your best interests at heart. And you need someone who has heavy-duty experience with your particular issue.

Now tell the truth: do your friends fit this particular job description?

For example, how unbiased can they be? Maybe your friends are disinterested, but maybe they, like my friends, have a whole brigade of hobby horses. One of my friends thinks it's wrong to do anything for money. Mention getting more money as one of your options and he'll immediately recommend something else. Another one of my friends always thinks you should "go for it." He can't help himself.

Look, I'm not saying that our friends are always biased about everything. I'm just saying that when it comes to serving as advisers our friends all too often have lurking biases that make it hard for them to see what's best for us.

And what about having your best interests at heart? Here too, you have to be careful. I'm sure your friends have the best intentions in the world. But a big decision will often change their lives even as it changes yours. If you're deciding whether to move across the country, your friend might have every reason of her own to want you to stay. (She might have every reason to want you to go!) If you're thinking of getting a divorce, your friend might want you in her life more as part of a couple than as a single person. She might not even be aware of this bias. But there might be a clear conflict of interest between what's good for you and what's good for her.

Friends are great. Just make sure you get the real experts you need.

Using experts

What is an expert? Whom should you go to when you need advice?

Suppose you're afraid you or someone you love has breast cancer. An expert is not someone who once had breast cancer. It's probably not even your own physician. The expert is the most unbiased, most highly credentialed, most respected person you can get ahold of when it comes to dealing with your particular issue. Go for the best expert you can dig up.

And get more than one expert. A lot of people are afraid of doing this because they're afraid of getting confused. But getting more expert input will accomplish a number of things:

First, if the experts are in agreement, then you can feel confident about which decision to make.

Second, if they all say different things (and usually they don't), then you know you really can make your own decision.

Third, by listening to what they think is important and to the questions they raise, you will actually learn how to think like an expert, and that will help you make a better decision.

I know a woman—a very good decision maker—who got a routine mammogram in which the first radiologist saw spots called micro-calcifications. These might be a sign, he said, of something that might be precancerous.

Instead of panicking she sought out breast-cancer specialists. First she went to a couple of surgeons with national reputations. Both recommended lumpectomies. Why? this woman asked. So you won't worry, the surgeons said.

Something was a little off. They were giving psychological reasons for a medical decision. But surgeons are trained to act. This woman realized that she didn't have a what-to-do problem, she had a what's-going-on-here problem. She needed a diagnostician, not a surgeon. She went to the top breast radiologist in her city.

He said, "Look, it's probably nothing, but even if it is something, it's overwhelmingly likely to be something very slow to develop. So let's watch and wait. We have nothing to lose." That's what she did. The micro-calcifications turned out to be nothing.

So find an expert, and make sure you find the right expert. Then trust the expert.

When you get in the way

People who feel bad about themselves worry about being devalued by the weight of an expert's opinion. If someone else is an expert, that means you're not an expert. The other person's expertise can feel like a putdown.

Check out your track record. If you can admit that you have a history of avoiding experts, it's probably because you feel somehow undermined in their presence.

You're not alone. But let's sort this out. The biggest reason people feel bad about themselves is that they've made more than their share of bad decisions. Staying away from experts will lead to still more bad decisions. Just think of it this way: Of course the experts you consult will be smarter and more knowledgeable than you are. That's why the greatest decision makers in the world go to experts. Don't you deserve the best?

You'll always hear people who make great choices say, "I talked to some people and got some really good advice." When it comes to steering the good ship What-the-Hell-Should-I-Do through the shoals of life, people who make great choices bring as many smart people on board with them as they can. And they listen to what the experts have to say.

Law #25

Keep an Open Mind

Are you caught in attitudes that keep you from seeing what's best for you?

L ET me tell you about how a good woman made a bad decision that killed her baby. If we understand how this well-intentioned woman went wrong, we can give ourselves the gift of a lifetime of good decisions.

When Sally got pregnant, she was overweight and in a high-risk category for having a first baby. A San Francisco obstetrician with top credentials told Sally that the risks could be managed, but only if Sally was very careful and followed orders.

But Sally was a believer in alternative healing and was untrusting of the medical establishment. Sally had what she thought was a "much better idea." She'd have her baby at home in San Francisco, where she could be attended by an inexperienced midwife who was her friend.

Sally was in her eighth month when she went into a prolonged labor. Hour after hour she sat at home with the midwife, her husband and friends, and music and incense. Her friends finally raised the issue of whether the baby was okay. The midwife listened with her stethoscope—the only equipment she had—and said that she kept hearing a heartbeat.

Sally wouldn't entertain any suggestions about going to the hospital. When her husband started begging her to consider it, she told him that if he was going to freak out, he would have to leave.

And on the labor went. Sally was clearly becoming utterly exhausted. Then the midwife panicked. She realized that the baby's heartbeat was growing weaker. She suddenly saw she was in over her head and knew that they had very little time to get Sally to a hospital, where she would probably need an emergency C-section.

Later the doctors concluded that the baby was dead before the ambulance even got to the hospital.

Sally had trouble admitting that her bad decision cost her baby's life. In Sally's version the baby wasn't meant to be born.

Sally's story is a sad case of what can happen when your attitudes distort your thinking. You will go down, and you may take people you care about with you.

Trapped in your attitudes

Every decision you will ever make is based on beliefs about how the world works. If your beliefs are more or less solidly based and true, you'll do fine. But every once in a while you and I get some faddish, crackpot notions in our heads that are all the more dangerous because they seem so perceptive and right at the time.

Usually you can tell that you're trapped in some attitude that will get you in trouble if it's your unquestioned rule of thumb. Take one particularly dangerous rule of thumb: always follow your heart. You haven't earned the right to use this as a rule of thumb if you haven't seriously and respectfully considered the alternative— always follow your head. And if you haven't considered the further alternative of following *both* your heart *and* your head.

We all know people like this, who took some simpleminded belief and rode it right up to the edge of the cliff and over. Here's a sample, just from my circle of friends.

There's the guy who became convinced that you can't go wrong investing in the emerging markets. That was where the action was. They're new, we're old. End of story. Like many slogans, there was a germ of truth in this. But I can't even begin to count the number of laws this guy was breaking with his simpleminded slogan. To take just three, he wasn't looking ahead to see how economic realities in the emerging markets would actually play out.

He wasn't doing what he needed to feel safe. And he wasn't accepting the way things really work. When the emerging markets tanked in 1998, he tanked with them.

There's the woman who wouldn't take hormone replacement therapy after menopause, even though she was in a low-risk group for breast cancer but a high-risk group for heart disease, and was experiencing many painful and disturbing symptoms. But it wasn't "natural." That was her attitude—"Natural is good"—and it drove a nail in the coffin of her marriage. The problem wasn't just that her symptoms were too much for an already shaky marriage to deal with. It was that her utter unwillingness to talk reasonably about her decision finally convinced her husband that he couldn't deal with her.

You would be amazed at how examples like these go on and on. An entrepreneur friend of yours won't let go of his belief in an obsolete technology and so dooms his business. Do you think that smart techno-businessmen are beyond this? I saw legendary Ken Olsen of Digital Equipment fame pound the table as he explained why there would never be a need or a market for personal computers. That was only fifteen years ago.

Finding your disabling beliefs

So right now stop thinking of weird beliefs and crackpot ideas as something that only other people hold. Let me beg you to consider the opposite possibility: that without realizing it you have ridden some attitude to defeat. Think about some of your bad decisions. Pick one. Now I'll bet you that one of the factors that led you into that dark alley where you got mugged by reality was some attitude of yours that you hadn't checked out and that wasn't really commonsensical. Underlying that was some crackpot idea.

Maybe you just got into a relationship with someone and it turned out to be a disaster. He was difficult, but you thought that being with you would straighten him out. There's a hobby horse lurking there—love conquers all; love is a wonder drug; love changes people.

Every time you talk about what led you to make a bad decision and say something like, "Well, I was just hoping . . ." or "Well, I just thought . . ." or "It's just that I was afraid that . . . ," you're probably referring to some belief you held that wasn't true or just didn't apply to that situation.

How do you protect yourself against this in the future?

Attitude insurance

You need insurance, and the problem is that you won't be able to see how your beliefs are limiting you. If it's a big enough decision for you to worry about, then it's important for you to call a meeting of your kitchen cabinet. . . . Wait a minute! You don't have a kitchen cabinet?

Well, maybe you do. I'm just talking about the smartest, savviest people in your circle of friends. Ask them to challenge your decision. Most important, ask them to challenge your reasons for making your decision.

This is what people who make good decisions do. This is what people who make bad decisions think they don't need to do, or think they're too busy to do.

Friends with a little bit of life experience and a lot of common sense are the only bulwark against being led unwittingly to disaster by crackpot ideas.

There's a concept I want you to have; it's a concept people who make good choices adhere to religiously. It's the concept of fresh air. Hobby horses fester and grow in closed minds. The fresh air of informed opinion prevents those hobby horses from taking on too much importance.

Do you remember the Y2K fears some people got so exercised about? It turns out that there were pockets of real Y2K panic among some social groups. Not just right-wing survivalists holed up in Montana. My mother-in-law in Florida lived in an apartment building filled with elderly men and women taking their money out of the bank to buy cartons of tuna fish and bottled water. They all talked to each other about how Y2K was going to bring the world to its knees. But there was no true fresh air—they didn't talk to anyone with different ideas.

I remember that I myself just didn't know. But I threw open the windows and talked to all the computer-type people I could. Particularly the computer people who were not making a living as Y2K consultants. Most felt that there might be a glitch or two, maybe a major but temporary glitch here and there, but nothing big or serious would happen.

And who turned out to be right?

Don't make a decision until you've aerated your reasons for making the decision. Any belief must be forced to survive the fresh-air test. And that means letting your beliefs be challenged by people who have ideas and perspectives that are different from yours. The more important your decision, the more important it is for you to talk to people who challenge your belief system.

I know this is hard. The more convinced you are of any belief in anything, the more you'll feel that talking to people with other points of view is a waste of time. But you haven't earned the right to say that, until you've aerated your beliefs and challenged them with other people's points of view. Only then can you know that you've saved yourself from the fatal errors we're led to when we wear blinders.

Law #26

Take Care of the Basics

Will your decision address your basic needs?

No matter what you decide, make sure your basic needs, basic responsibilities, basic concerns all get taken care of.

N APOLEON failed to do this. If he had consulted his mother about invading Russia, I'm sure she would've said, "But will you and your boys get enough to eat? And will you be warm enough when it's winter?"

What are the basics?

When I talk about basic needs, I'm talking about having enough sleep. Having money in the bank. Keeping close the people you love and the people you need. Taking care of your health.

Good decision makers make wonderful things happen by focusing on their basic needs.

One architect had fantasies about the house he wanted to live in, but he was just starting his career, as well as a family. He didn't have lots of money. He rented an inexpensive apartment in town to save on commuting expenses. The time he saved helped him jump-start his career. The money he saved helped him when it was time to start his own business. Now he does live in his dream house, because he did what he needed to do when it was time to do it.

So this law says that whenever you're about to make a big decision, and before you get carried away by dreams and opportunities, check in and ask how all the basics in your life will be affected by your decision.

Why we forget the basics

The most powerful telltale sign of a humility meltdown isn't arrogance. It's your explanation of why one of the basics no longer applies to you.

For example, everyone knows that everyone has to pay taxes. But one guy I know who refused to pay his taxes devised a plan for not getting caught: he lived his life completely on a cash basis. If you don't appear on their radar screens, he reasoned, the IRS can't shoot you down. But then he sold a screenplay to Hollywood for seventy thousand dollars. An accountant made it clear that he would have to file a return and report this income, and so he did. Of course he came under the scrutiny of the IRS.

Remember this story the next time you think some basic need or duty doesn't apply to you. It does apply. And be particularly careful with money. If you're making a decision that involves money in any way, don't risk a penny of what you need to live. For example, smart people start businesses with other people's money. Every business start-up is risky. There's too much competition out there, and there's no such thing as a surefire idea.

Basics are like the legs of a stool: take one away and you fall down.

Before you make a decision, take a basics inventory. Write down the basics in your life. What money do you need? Who are the important people in your life? What are your responsibilities? Do you have any health issues that need to be addressed?

Then ask yourself how the various options you're considering will affect the basics.

Any option that neglects the basics is bad no matter how seductive and glamorous it is. Any option that takes care of the basics deserves respect.

Law #27

Some of the Things You "Know" Are Wrong

Have you checked your facts?

RECENTLY NASA lost a multibillion-dollar Mars mission probe because in some of the data one group of scientists was using the English measurement system while another group was using the metric system. Things like this happen all the time. You assume you know the facts. But you don't check. An otherwise good decision goes down the tubes.

There's no permanent protection against this mistake. People who make great choices are at least aware of how easy it is to be mistaken about the facts you're most confident about. One of the smartest women I know once said, "The more important a decision is, the more I bet there's something I'm taking for granted that will turn around and bite me if I don't check it out."

You have to find out what facts must be true for your decision to work out right, then check those facts carefully.

Humility conquers all

Adam, a young man who'd inherited enough money to start a business, came to me with an idea for a children's book publishing company. These would be children's books for dyslexic readers.

I asked Adam, in an understated way, if he had a sense of whether parents and kids would be interested in his books.

Like a good businessman, Adam had done plenty of home-work. He knew how many dyslexic kids there were in America. He'd even done a small survey of parents of dyslexic kids, asking them if they would buy books designed for their kids.

Adam thought that the demand for books aimed at dyslexic children was intense. "Look, even if only 25 percent of dyslexic kids read my books," he said, "they will still be incredible hits." Adam was as confident as Coca-Cola was when they said their multimillion-dollar market research showed that people clearly preferred the new Coke to classic Coke.

Here's the question: had Adam really checked out his facts?

People had said they were interested. And it certainly seemed as though there was potentially a large market. But when we make big plans, they often rest on a narrow assumption. People who make good decisions pinpoint the assumption they need to check out. In Adam's case, he needed to check out whether all these people who seemed so interested would actually get excited enough about his books to buy them in numbers.

Adam never launched his series of books. He talked to a num-ber of dyslexic kids about the kinds of books they got excited about. They were the same books all kids get excited about. Dyslexic kids didn't want to be different.

Be humble. Know that there's plenty you don't know. Check things out as much as you can. If you need to act to get informa-tion, take small steps.

Let's look at the kind of humility that produces good decisions. Here are the actual voices of good and bad decision makers in one area of life after another.

Relationships

A good decision maker: "We seem great together, and she may really be the one, but we have to put in a lot more time to see how we are under real-life conditions."

A bad decision maker: "I just see the way she looks at me and the way all my friends think she's great. I just know she's perfect."

Money

A good decision maker: "Look, even full-time pros have trouble beating the averages. Why should I expect I can beat them? So let me move with caution, and if I detect any problems with an investment I can get out quickly."

A bad decision maker: "I've been seeing them talk about the market on TV for a long time and I know I can beat the big boys. There are all these ways their hands are tied. I'm a lot freer."

Office politics

A good decision maker: "My boss is really friendly with me, and that makes the atmosphere great. But in the end, a boss is a boss. She's not my equal—she can fire me. So I better be really careful about assuming that we can be close friends."

A bad decision maker: "My boss really likes me, and we tell each other everything."

In each of these three cases, the good decision maker never made assumptions about what he really knew. The bad decision maker just assumed he could peer through the water all the way down to the bottom of the sea.

We all make decisions based on facts we believe are true. But some facts are utterly crucial to a decision's success, and some of these "facts" are not actually true. Check out all the important facts your decision rests on.

Law #28

You Don't Have to Run from Risk

Do you know what the risks are and how to protect yourself?

SHOULD I eat this piece of pastry or not? Should I sell my company to these people who promise to let me stay on and run it?

No matter what it's about, to make a decision is to take a risk. Even if you think you're choosing between two different safe options, there's still the risk of choosing the less desirable option and regretting it afterward.

People who make bad decisions either don't see risks, ignore the risks they see, or become paralyzed by risk.

---

*People who make great choices **manage risk**. They see what the risks are and find a way to protect themselves.*

Begin with the understanding that risk *is* something that can be managed. If you've ever remembered to take an umbrella with you in the morning because you've heard it might rain, then you know about managing risk. It's all there inside you.

Julia, at forty-five, was one of the rare female mechanical engineers of her generation. She had recently been let go from a company that made computer-memory-storage devices, but with stock options and bonuses and a recent inheritance when her father died, she now had two hundred thousand dollars saved up. The question facing her was what to do with that money.

Julia was divorced, with two teenage children, and she hated being a mechanical engineer. Technology stocks were going through the roof, and Julia constantly read about how much money people were making—the kind of money she dreamed of making herself. But Julia felt that the money she had in the bank was all that stood between her and homelessness.

Julia decided to make a mental checklist to size up her risks. You can do it too. Here are the six steps to follow so you need never fear risk again.

Risk management 101

1. Understand what you really need
A fear is a need. Instead of being controlled by your fears, think carefully about what you need most, and let your most important need determine how you'll handle your risks.

Julia was afraid of losing her money, and she needed to sleep at night. She had to raise teenagers, and she felt she couldn't trust the job market at her age.

2. Get something in return for taking a risk
Being compensated for taking on risk is one of the fundamental principles of capitalism. Julia understood this and asked herself a very smart question. "Suppose I put all my money into these high-tech stocks. How well do most high-tech mutual funds do? Is it so much better than what you get from a money market account?"

Julia needed to feel that she'd be paid for her trouble. The question we all have to answer is, *How much pay for how much trouble?* Imagine four marbles in a pot, three white, one black. You're blindfolded. If you pick one of the white marbles, you get nothing. If you pick the black marble, you get a million dollars. Your chances of winning a million dollars are one in four, or 25 percent.

How much would you pay to play that game just one time? A buck? Sure! If you lose, so what? You bet only a buck.

But would you spend two hundred thousand dollars, the sum of Julia's savings? Now that's a tough question.

This is what Julia faced. The stock market had recently been climbing at a rate of 25 percent. But she *felt* as if she could lose it all, so the expected returns weren't payment enough for her. Too much uncertainty and too little hope of a big enough payoff to justify the uncertainty.

3. Make sure you have a way out

Knowing where the exits are, and knowing you can get to them in time, is the essence of feeling risk is manageable. Julia suddenly thought, Is this business of losing everything real? How many investments actually decrease to zero? If the market starts to fall, I can sell before I lose more than my entire two hundred thousand dollars.

4. Make sure you watch the situation

As Julia thought about having a way out, she realized she would have to watch what was going on in the market, but she wasn't sure how to do this, or how to predict an undesirable turn of events.

Once again Julia put her finger on something important. You can manage risk by watching very carefully what's going on. But you'd better be sure of what you're doing and be able to see trouble before trouble sees you. If you *can* really watch the situation, risk can dwindle to almost nothing.

5. Make sure you have the information you need

Julia asked herself the right question: "What exactly would I watch for if I watched the situation?"

Julia found the information she needed in a surprising place. She asked around for the names of some good, solid mutual funds that did well but that invested in safe companies. She then pretended that she had her money invested in one of these funds and followed it for a couple of weeks. Markets do fluctuate, and there were days when Julia lost a couple thousand dollars of her imaginary investment. But because these were funds that invested in safe, solid, maybe boring companies, the money she lost was less than what she would've lost if she'd invested in an index fund.

Then she asked herself how she felt about those losses, because that was the information she needed. She, in fact, was far less up-set than she'd expected to be. She said to herself, "I know what this fund has done, and I know the kinds of companies that are owned here. This is the best of America. Small fluctuations just don't bother me here."

Suddenly investing in safe mutual funds—conservatively man-aged, that traded a bit of return for a bit of safety—seemed like a perfectly manageable thing to do. Still Julia wasn't quite comfort-able. Then she presented herself with one more bit of wisdom.

6. Make sure you understand the risk of doing nothing

During all this talk about being afraid of what would happen to her money, something was happening to it right now. In a money market account, Julia was barely making more than the rate of in-flation. She did the math. At the current rate of inflation, in twenty-five years, her two hundred thousand dollars would've barely grown. She asked herself how she'd feel about that. The simple answer was not very good.

Doing nothing is risky too. And whenever you're facing a de-cision, you're already choosing one of your options, which is to keep on the way you've been keeping on, which is to do nothing. You haven't begun to manage risk until you've factored in the risk of doing nothing.

In the end, Julia put one hundred and seventy-five thousand dollars in a couple of safe mutual funds and kept the rest in a money market fund. This was very conservative, but her money would have a chance to grow.

Of course there's nothing spectacular about the choice that Ju-lia finally made. But how could there be? Julia wasn't a spectacular investor. People often confuse brilliance and talent with the ability to make great decisions. But they're very different. Brilliance and talent will allow you to see farther than other people and do things that other people can't do. But the financial world, the business world, the political world, and the scientific world are all filled with geniuses who make bad decisions and nongeniuses who make good decisions. Without any talent for money, Julia made a great decision. Not because she became a billionaire but because she knew what was important to her, she knew what she needed, and she accepted herself. Then she used this simple understanding to manage risk so she could both sleep at night and feel proud of herself.

Just because it is our tendency to freeze when we're scared, that doesn't mean that being immobile actually makes us safer. After all, fear is a response given to us by nature to get us to make a decision. Just watch an animal in danger. It will freeze only long enough to glimpse what seems like the best thing to do.

Know the six steps to managing risk and you will become a better decision maker.

Law #29

Following Through Makes Decisions Great

Will you do a great job carrying out your decision?

S OME people are intimidated at the thought of "making great decisions." They feel compelled to rise to some standard of brilliance and perfection that they just can't achieve.

Being intimidated like this is unnecessary. For one thing, it makes you stop trying. And that's disastrous. For another thing, as has become amply clear, the attitudes and thought processes needed to make a great decision belong to all of us. Anyone can do it.

Let's eliminate one more source of intimidation, which comes from the idea that a great decision has to be "great." Lots of people spend too much time searching for the perfect decision. If it doesn't hit the bull's-eye, they're not interested.

People who make great decisions don't operate this way. They work hard to make the best decision they can, but they don't spend a minute expecting each decision to be great. This may sound like a paradox, but it's true. People who make great decisions understand that perfection isn't possible when you take a leap into the dark.

Making sure you can carry it out

How then do they make great decisions when so often all they can do is make a pretty good decision, given what they have to work with? They do this by employing Law #29: *Following through makes decisions great.* They understand this:

Once you've made the best decision you can, you have to make your decision work by following through. You have to hang in there consistently and continue to improvise your way to victory.

Jason had been a struggling freelance sculptor for ten years, when suddenly a job possibility opened up to work as a full-time editor for a respectable art journal. It wouldn't pay a lot but certainly paid more than he'd made previously.

Should he take the job or not? That was Jason's big decision. What if he failed at the new job? His fragile ego couldn't take that. But a secure job like the one offered to him didn't come around every day. This is how we agonize over big decisions.

Fortunately Jason's wife came to the rescue. She asked him, "Which one do you think you'll be most successful at actually implementing?" That was the key. The best decision would be the one he could do the best job following through with.

So reviewing his choices, Jason realized that the new job was more likely to stress his family, and if he took it he'd be going *from* something he knew he was good at *to* something he wasn't so sure about. In the end he decided to continue to paint. It was a great decision because it took care of what was most important to him.

How to make it work

How do you follow through on a decision? Here's what to do.

1. Remember your original vision

This is the number one reason why people fail to follow through. They forget why they made the decision in the first place. You marry someone because you think he's wonderful. If that's your original vision, following through means celebrating his wonderfulness. But if you spend your energy trying to change him, that's a reversal of your original vision. It's following through on a vision of your mate as someone *not* wonderful. How can your decision succeed unless you follow through on the vision that caused you to make it in the first place?

2. Be persistent

Everything takes a lot longer than you think it will. Think about the search for a cure for cancer. Suppose, fifty years ago, that the government and the medical establishment had said, "Should we even try to find a cure for cancer? The cost of finding a cure will be so enormous that maybe it will be better if we put money behind treatment only."

Then suppose that someone else said, "No, let's look for a cure. We're smart and we have money and we'll work hard. Surely we'll be able to eliminate cancer by 1970 at the latest."

Inevitably, when optimistic predictions fail they generate equally pessimistic predictions—in this case, that there will never be a cure for cancer. (This is why having a hopeful heart and a cautious head is so important. Hope is good, in fact it's absolutely necessary, but if it's not tempered by caution the inevitable disappointments quickly sour hope into despair.)

But whether it's curing a deadly disease, launching an art career, finding the right formula for opening a successful new restaurant, or trying to heal a troubled relationship, people who make good decisions understand that it's the follow-through that ultimately yields rewards.

3. If you want to do a good job of following through, never stop troubleshooting

Most of us spend our lives in problem solving. The news here is that the problems you face are in fact the rungs of the ladder you climb to success. Success is built out of solved problems.

If the problems don't come to you, you should try to anticipate them, because they will come eventually. That's what troubleshooting is all about: looking for small problems before they become big ones. This can be a pain in the neck, because once you've worked hard to make your decision you'd like it to just run by itself.

Suppose you want to make a small investment in a residential rental property. You've run all the numbers, and they look good. An accountant experienced in real estate investing tells you it's a good deal. You have the makings of a good decision. But there's no such thing as a cash cow you can just ignore. Without troubleshooting, your good decision could turn into a disaster. Most important, you have to check out current tenants thoroughly and have a commitment to check out all future tenants diligently. A pain in the neck? Sure. But this kind of troubleshooting is the only way to follow through and make a good decision a great one.

4. Get feedback

You can't make your decision work unless you get feedback about what is going well and what's not. Good decision makers are hungry for this feedback, even when the words they hear are critical and problem laden. They understand that only when you get feedback can you follow through and act on problems that might make your decision turn sour.

But we don't all welcome feedback. Who wants criticism and bad news? Sometimes people are so insecure that they feel criticism will invalidate their decision. Suppose you get a new job, one you've been dreaming of for a long time. But you're nervous, because it's a big step up. The one thing you're hungry for, more than anything else, is being told you're doing a great job. And in part that hunger comes from your fear that maybe the decision to take this new job was a mistake.

This is the place where good and bad decision makers part company. No one wants criticism. Bad decision makers run away from the feedback they're afraid of getting. Good decision makers gulp and say, "I don't want to be criticized just starting out on this new job, but the only way I'll make a go of it is to get as much feedback as possible *as soon as possible.*"

5. Make alliances

We too often tend to keep our problems to ourselves because we don't want others to know we're struggling with a decision. But the right alliance with the right person at the right time—even if

it's just a worried phone call to a friend—may be all you need to
follow through on a decision. Think of your allies as co-investors
in your decision, even if they're just friends who wish you well.
They care, and because of that they will add input and energy to
keep you going during the period when you need to follow
through.

---

*Now you have what it takes to follow through on a decision and to
make it a great one.*

*Remember to hold on tight to your memory of your original vision.
That's your guide to making it all come out right.*

*Be persistent. Don't drop the ball, even if it feels as if they're try-
ing to take the ball away from you.*

*Never stop troubleshooting. The best trouble is the kind you find
before it finds you.*

*Get feedback. Every time you hear that you're doing it wrong is an
opportunity to do it right.*

*Make alliances. People who need people really are the luckiest
people. This is how they make their luck.*

Law #30

Make Decisions to Make Things Wonderful

Will you get something that's wonderful?

Everyone makes decisions to solve problems and stay out of trouble. People who make great decisions think about how to make things wonderful.

LET'S face it, most of us plod along, putting one foot in front of the other as we go through life. Sure, making bad decisions is a real danger. But failing to use our decisions to make things wonderful is a danger too. And when the opportunity slips by, it may never come again. You have to be on the lookout for this opportunity.

In the actual experience of making a decision, there's a window of opportunity that most people don't know about. I call this the decision gateway.

Let's say you own a house and you have no thought of moving. You're fine with the way things are. Then something happens. Maybe you get a new job. Maybe horrible people move in next door. Suddenly the possibility of getting a new house appeals to you. Before you know it, you're buying a house in a different neighborhood.

The decision gateway has closed. You locked yourself out of wonderful possibilities you never knew existed. You could've lived anywhere, in any kind of house. You could've bought a farm. You could've lived on a houseboat. You could've taken the money you're spending on a nice big house and gotten two nice, smaller houses. You could've joined the Peace Corps.

The decision gateway is that time when you're still free to ask yourself, "What would be wonderful here, and what can I do to make it happen?" And the decision gateway is precious because we narrow our search down far too quickly to what's attainable. Wonderful gets lost in the shuffle.

Take the example of careers. By the time you start sending out résumés, the decision gateway may be way behind you. You're looking for jobs you can get. At least you should be, because if you're sending out résumés for jobs that are only remote possibilities, you're probably in trouble. But it's never too late to ask yourself when it comes to work, "What would be a wonderful way for me to spend the next period in my life? What career would be a dream come true?"

On the lookout for wonderful outcomes

There are lots of ways we're distracted from thinking about the wonderful. For example, consider the Navy slogan "Join the Navy and see the world." Now that slogan's good for them because they need people to go on ships and be shuttled from one assignment to another. A few years later, well, you've seen the world, and then where are you? Suppose you'd said, "Seeing the world is good, but what would be *wonderful?*" Being an admiral? Becoming an oceanographer? Positioning yourself so you can join the CIA? Getting a career that will help you earn a good living for the rest of your life?

The point is, though, when you're in the decision gateway, before you sign up with the Navy first think about what would be wonderful for you.

Think about everyday life in corporate America. Most people who work for corporations would in fact make different choices if at the very beginning they had said, for example, "I want to be CEO and run the whole thing."

You think it doesn't make a difference to begin by shooting for the moon? *Working Woman* magazine—and pay attention, guys, because this applies just as much to you—recently had an article about women who are poised to be the very next CEOs. What brought them to the top—talent? hard work? Forget that. Most people have talents and work hard. It was this law of wonderfulness that did the trick. These women in this survey got to the top because way back when they were in the decision gateway they opted for jobs with line responsibility, where they were not only in charge of something but had to show a profit. They opted out of those staff jobs that didn't put them in the position to get to the top.

If a decision is important enough for you to worry about, then you deserve to anticipate something wonderful coming from it. That's what great decision makers have in their heads. That's what bad decision makers keep forgetting.

A guy I know was struggling to write the great American novel for fifteen years. He rarely got much writing done because he was always struggling to figure out what he really wanted to say. The whole thing was self-indulgent and unfocused.

But the real problem was that he wasn't thinking of something wonderful—he just wanted to write a book. Here's how he turned things around. He asked himself, "What if I wrote a best-seller?" Now the truth is that to write a best-seller you only have to write a book that appeals to a very small percentage of the American book-buying public. If you write a book, for example, that's bought by 1 percent of American adults, that's actually a big best-seller.

My friend got much of what he wanted. He wrote his book, it was successful, he made money, and he got a chance to write another book. Was it a best-seller? Almost. But that's not what this law is designed for—making every detail of your dreams come true. It's about getting more "wonderful" than you'd ever thought you'd get, certainly more than you would've gotten if you just went plodding along hoping for something halfway decent to happen.

Is it safe to shoot for the moon?

There's another side to this story of shooting for the moon. It's the fear of disappointment you see in so many people. Every one of us has had fond hopes that were dashed. Dreams that never came true no matter how hard we tried.

And disappointment hurts. So it feels like wisdom to avoid setting yourself up for disappointment. It feels like a kind of gritty street wisdom to say, "Be realistic. A bird in the hand is worth two in the bush."

How do you reconcile these two, realism and the search for something wonderful? You reconcile them by bringing a realistic attitude to your search for something wonderful. Shoot for the moon, but don't get caught up in your own hype. Realistically, you don't shoot for the moon because you're hoping to get the moon. Anyone who counts on having all his dreams come true is a damned fool. But half a dream come true is better than none.

Some bad decision makers are wildly unrealistic. Some are crippled by fear of disappointment. People who make great decisions ask themselves what would be a wonderful outcome before they lock themselves into a limited set of options. And then they remain open in their minds and hearts to whatever happens. They shoot for the moon and understand that that's the only way to get halfway to the moon. They're not disappointed when their dreams don't come true, because they understand that dreams are only fuel for making good things happen.

They say, "I'm taking the road where wonderful things happen. I'll never stop asking myself what I think will be wonderful. I'll never stop basing my decisions on my dreams. I'll never let disappointment blind me to how far my dreams have taken me."

The Law of Wonderfulness says that you should never settle when it comes to making a decision. If you'd look your best friend in the eye and say, "This is a very important decision for me," don't decide until you're convinced you've created the possibility of getting something wonderful.

It's Not the End, It's the Beginning

HERE's one more secret of people who make great decisions. It's the same secret shared by people who come up with great ideas and people who write great songs.

The secret is that you make great things happen by making things happen. You want to write great songs? Write songs. You want to make great decisions? Make decisions.

Start today. Decide something today. Maybe not something momentous, but decide something that matters to you. Just do it.

And make another decision tomorrow. Look forward to making a fairly big decision within the next week. Give yourself a month in which to make some really big decision you've been putting off for a long time.

Be a person who makes decisions. After all, you now know that you have everything you need to be a great decision maker. The thirty laws here—they're yours, not mine. They came out of the lives and minds and hearts of everyday people. They're not exotic ideas. They're answers you can find inside yourself because each one is something you already believe, something you've already acted on in other parts of your life.

Think of the thirty laws here as permission to be yourself. As long as you remember not to violate them, you'll do great.

All you need now is practice. The more you make decisions, the better you'll get at it.

If you should ever experience a pang of doubt, just remember that you yourself bring the most important ingredient. You care about making good decisions. Your caring gives you the foundation for a lifetime of good decisions.

Index

About the Author

Charles Foster is director of The Chestnut Hill Institute in Boston. His background is an unusual combination of training and practice as a psychotherapist, business consultant, and researcher. For twenty-five years he has worked both in a clinical and a business setting to help people make great decisions. Dr. Foster's work has been guided by two principles. First, he passionately believes that you help people most by showing them how to build on their strengths. Second, the best solutions to the problems we struggle with can be found by studying what successful people do on their own. Dr. Foster has made numerous TV and radio appearances and was featured in a recent ABC News prime-time special with *20/20*'s John Stossel. He has a Ph.D. from the Heller Graduate School of Advanced Studies at Brandeis University and an M.B.A. from the Boston College Graduate School of Management. Charles Foster got married at age eighteen to Mira Kirshenbaum, with whom he has collaborated on nine books. They have been married for thirty-five years and have two grown daughters who are busy inventing the future.